Underst[a]
Chaos Magic

Jaq D Hawkins

To Danny,
Enjoy the Chaos,
Jaq D Hawkins

Understanding Chaos Magic

©1996 Jaq D Hawkins

ISBN 1 898307 93 8

Cover design & illustration by Daryth Bastin

Published by:

Capall Bann Publishing
Freshfields
Chieveley
Berks
RG20 8TF

Dedicated to my dear husband,
Jeremy,
and to my daughter.
Wendy Lefay

Acknowledgments

I would like to thank the special people who have contributed support and information for this book, beginning with the multitudes who have continually asked me, "What is Chaos Magic?" Special thanks are due to Ray Sherwin, Charles Brewster, Lola Babalon and Hendrik Bohm for their contributions to the history of the IOT. I would also like to thank Charles Nemo for allowing me liberal use of his extensive occult library, Cheryl Fluder and Liz Eastwood for re-typing the entire manuscript out of the goodness of their hearts and Sue Fawcett for allowing them to do so on company time, and Nick Frost and James Pengelly for their individual philosophical insights which have affected various sections to this book.

Special thanks are sent out to Mr. Kenneth Grant, for his patient answers to my never ending stream of questions about his old friend, Mr. Austin Osman Spare.

February,   1994

The Author

Jaq D. Hawkins began to take an interest in new age subjects at the age of nine, after being exposed to astrology through an aunt and noticing strange phenomena in her life and those of other family members. By the age of thirteen she was practicing ritual magic, although she would not begin proper study with others who shared her interest for another two years.

After more than three decades of study in a variety of magical directions and traditions, her path brought her to Chaos, where she has become known among a select group of magicians who share an interest in this area of magic. Her articles on the subject of Chaos Magic have appeared in several new age magazines, including Mezlim where she is a regular contributor.

Ms. Hawkins is currently living in North Yorkshire. She shares her adventure through life with her daughter, who is having a very interesting childhood.

Introduction

Chaos Magic is the newest and fastest growing area of hands-on practical magic available to the modern magician. It is an area of study which disposes of the need for religion, prepackaged philosophy and superstition in the use of magic. The Chaos Magician seeks to understand the natural laws behind the workings of magic, and the reasons behind the use of ritual in the performance of a magical working.

Chaos magic leaves the practitioner free to establish his/her own ideas of method, ethics and appropriate uses of magic. It is magic for the liberated free thinker who is able to go beyond the teachings of any book to the outermost reaches of imagination in the creation of one's own magical world.

It is magic based on the concept of the primal creative force itself, a realm of infinite probability. Creative Chaos is a subject most useful to experienced magicians who can determine for themselves the risk factor in the release of powerful spells that work.

While the actual practice of this form of magic is recommended for the experienced magician, the subject is of interest to anyone who may benefit from the understanding of the way our minds can affect our environment.

Chaos Magic is magic based on natural laws, many of which are only beginning to be understood by the scientific community. Stripped of superstition and religious bigotry, it is a realm where fact meets theory, and results are the objective.

It is magic which transcends tradition and dogma; A journey toward results rather than hierarchical megalomania. It is as useful and effective for the individual as it is for a group, and infinitely adaptable to the needs of the many or the few. Any and all methods are allowed and encouraged, the only requirement is that it works.

Chaos Magic is the 'cutting edge' of modern magic. It is on the minds and lips of magic users of all descriptions and in many parts of the world. As we learn more and more about the nature of magic and reality, we are beginning to realize that behind all forms of magic, are the natural laws of Chaos.

Notes on Chaos Magic

Understanding Chaos Magic is the first book to bring the concepts and ideas of this new and exciting area of magic to the general public. Until now, most books about this subject have been released in limited editions, available only to a select few. Those which have been available to the public have been largely specialized and riddled with terms which are unfamiliar to the average reader.

Understanding Chaos Magic explains and demystifies the natural laws of chaos in magic, in simple terms that the average person can easily follow. The catch phrases of chaos science and the concepts behind them are translated into simple language, as well as the meanings of this area of science to magic.

This is the first book to address all of the elements which comprise this area of magic in an easy to read format. It covers the history of what is known as Chaos Magic today, the theory and philosophy behind the workings of magic itself.

Also included are the new methods of performing magical ritual which are growing in popularity across the spectrum of different magical traditions. These are explained in a short, concise style which will leave the reader with an overall understanding of the subject of Chaos Magic, and of the nature of magic in general.

With the rapid growth of interest in chaos science as well as Chaos Magic across a wide spectrum of the new age community today, the question, "What is it?" is continually on the lips of the curious, the interested, and especially the intuitive among us, who can see that something revolutionary has taken hold of our understanding of the way things work in our world and of the way that science relates to natural magic.

Understanding Chaos Magic seeks to answer the questions in the simplest possible way, allowing the reader to choose whether to delve more deeply into the specializations of Chaos, or to be content with an understanding of what all the fuss is about. It is a beginning to the understanding of the nature of the magic of, and in, creation.

Table of Contents

In the Beginning...

The word 'chaos', according to the Oxford English Dictionary, means; "1. A gaping void, yawning gulf, chasm, or abyss. 2. The 'formless void' of primordial matter, the 'great deep' or 'abyss' out of which the cosmos or order of the universe was evolved." There are additional definitions, including a reference to disorder and confusion, but magic and confusion do not make very good bedfellows. In referring to Chaos Magic, the relevant definition is the second one. The "primordial matter", sometimes referred to as "infinite probability" by Chaos Magicians, is the well spring of that power which is called magic. Chaos Magic is the study of how to tap that source, and the natural laws which direct it.

It is well known that things once considered to fall within the realm of magic have become accepted sciences as humankind has learned to understand how things work. Alchemy was a precursor to modern chemistry; Astrology brought interest to the movement of stars in the sky, resulting in the study of astronomy. The mysteries of alchemy and astrology still hold the interest and imaginations of many people today, despite the common person's ability to understand much of the workings of nature behind these things. There is still much which cannot be explained by science. There is phenomena which are referred to as "supernatural" or "paranormal" of many kinds which are observed frequently. What was once dismissed as 'superstition' by educated people is more and more frequently being studied by professional researchers. Some major universities have even opened parapsychology departments.

There are still many things which science cannot explain. Researchers continue to try to find rational explanations for things regarded as magic, meanwhile, there are still people in cultures which practice some form of magic as part of a cultural religion, in some cases performing unexplainable feats which the educated scientist is unable to understand or duplicate. In our educated western societies, we have an increasing number of people who are practicing neo-pagan religions, learning what they can about magic from history and existing 'primitive' societies, unconcerned about scientific explanations. There are also people who study alone or in small groups. Many of these people are well educated in the sciences, yet look beyond known science to those things which are not yet understood, and are commonly referred to as "unusual phenomena". Things which still fall into the realm of magic.

The belief in genuine magic has been growing in our society since the revival of interest in new age subjects in the 1960's. Oddly, it has recently come to light that this same time period saw the beginning of a scientific revolution which would contribute to the serious study of the workings of magic. New versions of pre-Christian religions have flourished over the past three decades, and a general acceptance of things like the natural energy in crystals and other 'new age' beliefs have become widespread, even among well educated people who realize the difficulty in trying to apply the 'scientific method' to experiments in this area. Magical Orders have also seen a revival of interest over the years. Ceremonial magic, with all its formalism and tradition, seems to appeal to a very intellectual sector of society.

Outside of the religious celebrants of the form of magic commonly referred to as 'witchcraft', and the historic Orders of esoteric tradition, there have always been a few renegades and individualists who would practice alone rather than attempt to fit in to the structures of one of the existing magical groups or societies. A few have written books and passed ideas down to new generations. As the freedom of the 1960's affected all of society, it also brought a new freedom into the practice of magic. More people saw magic through an individualistic perspective. By the 1970's, a synchronicity had formed that would combine magic, science and individuality. It was time for a new perspective of magic which could only result in creative chaos.

A History of Chaos

The chaos principle in magic is far from new. It is only the title, Chaos Magic, which has come to us in this century. Indeed, any magic which brings about something from apparently nothing is in keeping with the use of the primal chaos creation principle. The methods change somewhat with different cultures in how to utilize this creative energy, but the physical principles remain the same.

Some of the more well known methods today, such as sigilization, have been used for centuries in some form or another. For example, the Norse Runemasters sometimes used their symbols in much the same way that modern magicians use written sigils in ritual. Runes are best known in modern times as a method of divination. This sells them short as they are also quite potent in the purpose of casting spells.

The word 'chaos' in relation to magical workings is first associated with a magician and artist by the name of Austin Osman Spare. Later, about 20 years after the death of Spare, the term 'Chaos Magick' becomes equated with a new magical Order called the Illuminates Of Thanateros, or IOT.

Wynne Road in Lambeth

While the IOT is still in healthy operation at the time of this writing, splinter groups and individual Chaos Magicians have taken this area of magic into as many new directions as there are repeating designs on a fractal diagram. Mr. Spare probably would no recognize his own influence on what is now called Chaos Magic.

The Nescient Father of Chaos

Austin Osman Spare was an artist and magician. His art and magic were very closely intertwined in his life. He was born on the 30th day of December, 1886 at midnight, in the small town of Snow Hill which has since been swallowed up in the London suburbs. Spare came from humble roots. His father was a London policeman, often working the night shift. He was the first son (although the middle child) in a family of five children.

There is little doubt that finances were stretched thin in the Spare family, yet when the young Spare showed an unusual aptitude for drawing, the family managed to find the funds to send him to art school. At the age of 13, he left school to serve an apprenticeship in a stained-glass works, but continued his education at Art College in Lambeth (South London) in the evenings. During this time he won a scholarship to the Royal College of Art and began serious artistic study.

Opposite: Last abode of the artist and magician - the basement apartment where Austin Osman Spare last conjured and drew his spirits was at Number 5, Wynne Road. The apartment, and indeed the section of the road itself, no longer exists as the map sections on the following pages show. The photographs show the block of flats which now occupy the space which was once the dwelling place of perhaps the greatest magician of all time.

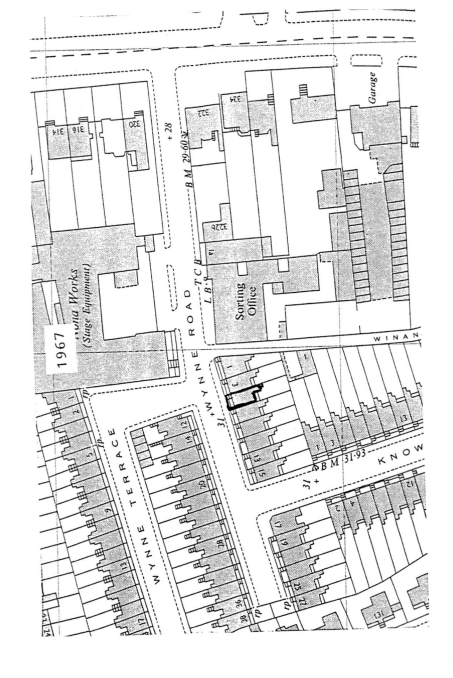

Wynne Road still existed as late as 1967

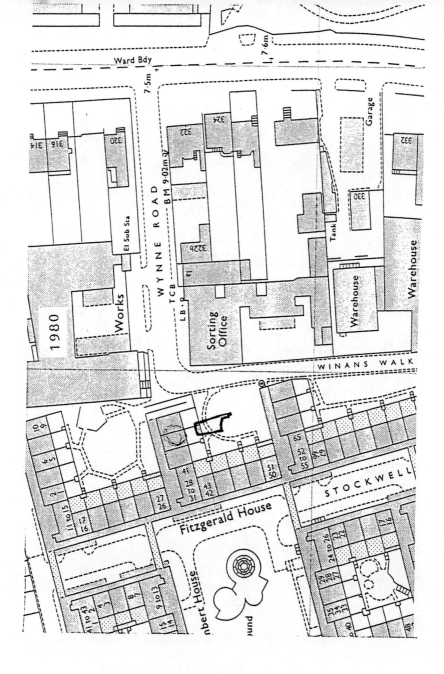

In 1980, Wynne Road has been shortened and new flats built
on the site

The turning which once went straight on

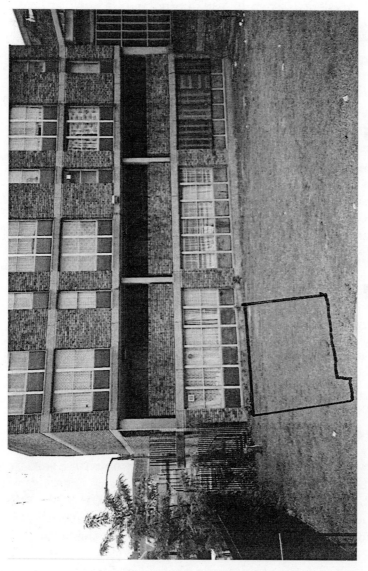

Just on the left, a patch of grassy lawn covers the spot where remnants of A. O. Spare's basement apartment may still lie buried

Spare very quickly gained popularity in the art world. He exhibited his first picture in 1904, at the age of 17, in the Royal Academy. Then in 1905 he published his first book, *Earth Inferno*. It was primarily meant to be a book of drawings, but included commentaries that showed some of his insight into the workings of the human mind and his spiritual leanings.

Spare's drawings were unusual to say the least, often depicting human figures in grotesque postures or semi-human spirit forms which he was able to visualize. In the Foreword to Earth Inferno, it is explained that, "The Text is not intended to fully explain, and the reader must be left to place his own interpretation upon the illustration, which is not grotesque for the sake of originality, but representative of the 'inferno' of Earth emblematical in Art."

Already, before even looking upon the drawings or words of Spare, one is being entreated to begin an independent thinking process leading to personal interpretation of what one will find. This is quite typical in the works of Spare, both in drawings and the written word. Spare continually tells us that we have the ability to think for ourselves. A seemingly simple statement, yet a concept that is very difficult for a large percentage of our conformist society to truly grasp.

The word 'Chaos' first appears in connection with Spare in this book. The title of the first full page size drawing is, "DESTINY, HUMANITY, and THE CHAOS OF CREATION." It would be presumptuous to attempt to interpret the drawing itself for the reader as the section of the Foreword which I have just quoted clearly indicates that each of us must interpret these drawings in our own way. The reference to chaos in connection with creation brings our attention back to the definitions of the word chaos, as quoted in the first part of this book.

Chaos Magic is the art of forming the unformed energies of creative chaos into a pattern leading to the outcome of the magician's desire. Understanding the nature of unformed or undirected aetheric energy is at the heart of the most basic of magical teachings.

It is in *Earth Inferno* that Spare first refers to "Kia" which is Spare's symbol for the cosmic self, which uses Zos, his identification for himself as body, mind and soul in connection with sorcery, as its field of activity. He also makes references to himself, to ambition, to Heaven and Hell.

It seems a lot of ground to cover in a first book, especially one classified under 'Art' rather than 'Philosophy', but that is one of the things which distinguishes Spare as an original thinker. To him, art is philosophy, as well as magic. The truth of this has become much more apparent to the generations of artists, magicians, and philosophers since Spare.

Another drawing in *Earth Inferno* is titled simply, 'CHAOS'. It faces a page which contains quotes from Dante's Inferno, and from *The Book of Revelation*, as well as his own caption, "The perpetual youth of man arises, Draws aside the curtain-Faith (a token of humanity's LIMITED knowledge), and exposes the inferno of THE NORMAL."

Above the drawing itself, which depicts a man drawing aside a curtain to see a mass of human bodies writhing together in various postures, is the entreaty, "Oh! come with me, the KIA and the ZOS, to witness this extravagance." Opening the book to these two pages exposes the reader to an insight of the human drama as only a philosopher can step aside and look upon it.

The following two pages contain a caption and drawing titled, "THE DWELLERS ON THE THRESHOLD", which immediately brings the fictional stories of H.P. Lovecraft to mind, as many of his stories focus on unseen entities that he often refers to in this way. Spare refers to "Creating a CHAOS of reflection" in dwelling on the threshold ourselves, inferring that we are our own demons. The last drawing in this book is titled, "Knowledge and Illusion". This looking beyond illusion to ascertain the truth of existence summarizes the message of the book, if a single message is to be conveyed. Spare's drawings and commentaries on youth and blindness unmasked throughout this book leave plenty of room for reflection within and interpretation through the mind of each reader.

During the time that this first book was published, the young Spare was residing with a novelist, the Reverend Robert Hugh Benson. One of the more unusual stories one often hears about Spare's magical conjurings occurred while Spare was on a walk with Benson. It was a clear Summer day, and as a joke Benson suggested that Spare try some rainmaking. Spare, always willing to oblige, drew a sigil on a scrap of paper and concentrated his will upon it. Within a few minutes a cloud formed overhead and drenched them both.

There are several stories of Spare's ability to achieve instant results with this sort of magic, as well as incidences of conjuring spirits and ghosts. There are also references to familiar spirits in some of Spare's writings and in Kenneth Grant's writings about him, including the spirit of an American Indian named Black Eagle who

Spare believed did his automatic drawings, sometimes even while he slept. A drawing of Black Eagle appears in *Images and Oracles of Austin Osman Spare*, by Kenneth Grant (Frederick Muller, Ltd, London, 1975), who knew Spare for many of his later years.

Many of Spare's more grotesque drawings were of entities that he was able to visualize. Spare's second book of drawings, *A Book of Satyrs* (pronounced satires), contained thirteen of his unique and potentially disturbing drawings. This book was published in 1907 and has been copied in privately released editions in recent years. The characteristic commentaries of *Earth Inferno* were not included in this book. The drawings were accompanied only by captions. The drawings, however, do seem to speak for themselves. The symbolism contained in most of Spare's drawings requires careful study and analysis to be truly appreciated.

One point which is noteworthy to those who would study Spare's art is that his self-portraits, of which there are several included in his books of drawings, depict a rather wild and untamed image of a man quite unlike the only actual photograph of Spare in his youth that I have ever seen. The photograph, circa 1908, is the frontplate for the book, *The Bookplate Designs of Austin Osman Spare*, compiled by Robert Ansell (The Bookplate Society in association with Kerridwen Press, 1988). It was published in a limited edition of 500 copies. It shows a young man wearing a suit, arms folded and his naturally curly hair nicely combed. The features of his face are well defined and almost delicate. A closer look reveals that his collar is somewhat rumpled. One may infer that this is a carefully posed photograph that the young Spare submitted to for some official purpose, either as a student or as an artist. Close examination of the eyes shows the only similarity to later photographs of Spare. The eyes are intense and seem to look both through and beyond the observer at once. These are the eyes of a visionary, one who will not be fully appreciated by his peers in his lifetime.

The self-portraits by comparison, show a decadent image, with much heavier features and a rougher appearance than this photograph. The hair is wild and curly while the eyebrows meet at the bridge of the nose, slanting upward demoniacally. Some of these images were drawn while Spare was still quite young, yet resemble his later photographs much more than this one photograph of his youth.

At the age of seven, Spare was befriended by a sorceress named Mrs. Paterson, whom Spare referred to as his "second mother". This woman was to be a great influence on the young Spare. It was said that she could change her appearance from that of an old woman to that of a young temptress at will, along with other odd powers. One drawing that Spare made of her is reputed to change before the eyes of those looking upon it.

In 1908 Spare held an art exhibition at Bruton gallery. By this time he had become very popular among the 'smart set' in London, the art collectors and dandys of the time. About 1910 he joined Aleister Crowley's Argentium Astrum, an occult Order of a similar nature to the Golden Dawn.

This association did not last long. Spare had begun work on his most well known book, *The Book of Pleasure*, and had his own ideas concerning the practice of magic. This book was first published in 1913, but is more easily found today in reprint editions, most often limited to 500 or 1000 copies. It is considered his most important magical work,

26

and includes detailed instructions for his system of sigilization and the well known "death postures".

Some of the drawings in this book are more detailed than previously published works. The writing goes into deeper detail of Spare's philosophy as well. He has much to say here about human hypocrisy, outward show of religion and even some magical groups and the meanings of true personal freedom and power. It is also in this book that Spare describes his "neither-neither" principle and that of "free belief".

These concepts are important keys to magic, and ones that should be read in their original form to be fully appreciated. This is where many students of magic find that they must shift their thinking processes if they are to find value in what may appear to some as bizarre rambling. In fact, every word and sentence of this particular book is an alchemist's goldmine of the 'secrets' of magic that many spend lifetimes trying to discover, yet the meanings are clear only to those who have already achieved a similar mindset to that which Spare tries to describe within these pages.

In 1916, Spare joined the army and served as an official war artist during the first World War. He was posted to Egypt which had a great effect on him. The animal-headed gods and magical religion of Ancient Egypt could hardly fail to appeal to the insightful nature of the artist and mystic. During the second World War, Spare suffered an injury when his home in London was devastated by a bomb-blast which paralyzed his right side. Naturally, this caused him a great deal of depression as he believed for some time that he would never draw again. However, within six months time he had recovered the use of his right arm and began to learn to draw all over again. This incident is related in detail in the book, *Images and Oracles of Austin Osman Spare*. Grant credits Spare's personal elementals and familiars for the speed of his recovery. He also points out that Spare's memory was affected by the blast, and that many of the drawings done during this recovery period were dated many years earlier.

In 1921 Spare published *The Focus of Life*, which is another book of drawings which includes his unique and magical commentaries. The word 'chaos' comes in again here in relation to the normality of chaos in the natural order of things and in self, "The more chaotic--the more complete I am". Spare speaks mostly to himself as Zos in this book. He has become the confident philosopher and has much to say to us, if we are able to listen. He speaks here of existence, of sex, of ecstasy and sensation. Spare seems to continue many of the ideas from Book of Pleasure here, about self-love, belief and the "chaos of the normal".

From 1921 to 1924 he was at the height of his artistic success, then, in 1924, the outward successes of his artistic career conflicting with the philosopher within brought him to a turning point. Spare had become disenchanted with the trendy artistic friends and benefactors with whom he had been so popular. He wrote another book, titled *The Anathema of Zos*, in which he effectively excommunicated himself from these people, flaunting their hypocrisies in their faces. He returned to South London and obscurity to find the freedom to develop his philosophy, art and magic.

There is little known about the activities of Spare during this time. He lived in a small basement apartment, caring little for money or fame. He made his living drawing portraits of the common people in the local pub and selling them for small amounts of money. He was offered larger sums on occasion but refused to accept them. Although he wasn't publishing during this time, Spare continued to write.

In 1947 Spare met Kenneth Grant and became more involved with other occultists of the time. From 1948 to 1956 he began work on a definitive Grimoire of the Zos Kia Cultus which is referred to in his various writings. This is unfinished and is being synthesized from Spare's papers by Kenneth Grant, who inherited Spare's papers.

Austin Osman Spare died in May of 1956. Most of his unpublished papers went into the hands of Kenneth Grant who has published much of the material in *Images and Oracles of Austin Osman Spare*, but there remains some unpublished material which Grant intends to publish when time from his Typhonian series allows.

More recently in 1992, Fulgar Press, London, has released a limited edition of texts and drawings apparently composed by Spare during the early 1950's. The title is *Axiomata and The Witches Sabbath*. The combined texts are printed back-to-back. Included is a preface written by Robert Ansell, who is known to have collected and published bookplates drawn by Spare. Collectors of Spare's works have had varying comments to make about the written text of these books, but all agree that there is quite a difference from his earlier works. The nature of this difference I leave to readers of these works to decide for themselves.

After his death, Spare's published works did not entirely disappear, but became collector's items among a few magicians in the U.K. The material began to resurface in the early 1970's in small occult magazines. In issue #4 of a magazine called Agape, a magician by the name of Lionel Snell published a facsimile of *The Anathema of Zos* along with an essay titled Spare Parts which was a commentary on *The Book of Pleasure*. This essay is reproduced in a collection of articles by and about Spare called *Excess Spare*, which was recently available from a nonprofit group known as Thee Temple Ov Psychic Youth, or T.O.P.Y.

It also appears in another collection of Spare's works titled, *The Collected Works of Austin Osman Spare*, which was edited and compiled by Christopher Bray. This was published by Bray's own publishing company, The Sorcerer's Apprentice Press (Leeds, 1986, second revised edition) in limited editions. This volume contains all of Spare's previously published books except *The Book of Satyrs*, as well as a very interesting introduction by Christopher Bray and the Lionel Snell essay already mentioned. Reprints of Spare's writings surface periodically in a number of forms. A very complete collection was released in 1993 by Mandrake Press (Thame, England), titled *From the Inferno to Zos*, edited and compiled by A R Naylor. This volume was released in three editions, limited full leather and one-quarter leather collector's editions plus a trade hardback edition which is more accessible to the average income student of magic.

Lionel Snell published a book in 1974 titled *SSOTBME* (Nigel Grey Turner, Surrey, 1979) which reflects the idea of the world being shaped by our perception of it, and other ideas common to much of Spare's writings and modern chaoist philosophy. It is very likely that the publishing of this material contributed to the interest in Spare by today's academic magicians of various persuasions. That Spare's material and the books written by Snell influenced the magicians who were to form the Illuminates of Thanateros, or IOT, a few years later is commonly known.

The word 'Thanateros' is a conjunction made from the Greek 'Thanatos' which means death, and 'Eros' which means sex. The word can also mean poison. Those familiar with magical symbolism will recognize the significance in these meanings. Death, the destruction principle, and sex, the re-creative principle are very basic concepts in magic. It is the old symbolic tearing down of the old to make room for the new, as the Phoenix who is destroyed in flame yet rises made anew from the ashes. The relationship between the concepts of procreation and death were a strong element in the writings of Austin Osman Spare. Poison, for all its sinister reputation, is akin to medicine as any doctor or herbalist knows. The most powerful healing drugs include ingredients which are poisonous by themselves, in quantities which will kill the disease without destroying the host. In magic, it is necessary to destroy the disease of preconceived beliefs in order for the soul to be free to perform.

A Societal Bifurcation

The Illuminates of Thanateros began in the late 1970's in England. A young Englishman by the name of Peter J. Carroll was living in an area of South East London called Deptford, best known for the 'Press Gangs' who recruited for the Royal Navy by knocking unsuspecting strangers over the head, after which they awoke on a ship at sea, and for being the area where the Punk fashion originally took root in London. For all its rough edges, this area attracted an interesting collection of artists and intellectuals, many of whom were involved in various aspects of the 1960's revival of magic and interest in new forms of music and philosophy.

Most of the focus of magic in England at that time was either on the Wiccan traditions, with all of their religious overtones, or on Thelemic Ceremonial Magick and the very traditional organizations which are associated with it.

Mr. Carroll was one of those who had more eclectic ideas about magic in general at that time and was familiar with the writings of Austin Osman Spare. Carroll was a regular contributor to a magazine called *The New Equinox* which was edited and published by another creative young Englishman named Ray Sherwin. Mr. Sherwin and Mr. Carroll became acquainted and there were frequent visits between them. At first this was in London, where it was not uncommon for a group of magicians to gather for social occasions at a block of flats in Deptford known as Speedwell House.

It is difficult to pinpoint an exact moment when Chaos Magic of the IOT flavour began, but one significant occasion was the 'Deptford Olympics Goat Roast' which coincided with the Montreal Olympics in 1976. This was, as the title suggests, a sports day held in a waste ground behind Speedwell House, followed by a grand barbeque party complete with spitted goat, live punk ensemble and a pyrotechnic display provided by some of the local anarchists.

Peter Carroll was working on a magical treatise titled *Liber MMM* during this period, which was later published by Ray Sherwin as *Liber Null*. After a trip to the East, Carroll spent some time living in Yorkshire where he spent a fair amount of time in the company of Mr. Sherwin who had written and published a few books of his own, including the underground classics *Theatre of Magick* and *The Book of Results*. *The Book of Results* was re-issued by Revelations 23 Press, Sheffield, in 1992. Sherwin and

Carroll had many a conversation on the subject of magical theory and the situation of magical groups in England. They shared a dislike for hierarchical organizations, which led to discussions of the plausibility of a non-hierarchical magical Order. At some point during this time, the two of them became the original IOT. Carroll had suggested the name, which he may have had in mind while working on his earlier writings. It was during this time in Yorkshire that he wrote *Psychonaut*, which was later published in the same volume as Liber Null by Samuel Weiser, Inc. An ad was placed in The New Equinox to recruit members, and the group began to take form.

One very noteworthy point about the early members of the IOT is that they were mostly University educated. Peter Carroll had been a Chemistry major, Ray Sherwin studied Theology and has taught English at Cairo University. Another of the early members, Charles Brewster, was a Geology major who subsequently wound up as an instrument technician working for the research group at University College whose photon detector identified the first 'black hole'. During this same time period, unknown to these bright young magicians, a man by the name of Mandelbrot was developing chaos mathematics at the IBM Research Center in Yorktown Heights, New York. The melding of chaos math and science, and Chaos Magic, was still to come. It would be Peter Carroll who would first notice the relationships between the two.

The New Equinox advertisement appeared in 1977. The issue also contained an editorial rant written by Ray Sherwin encouraging academic magicians to get on with magic and get some results rather than spending their time pondering "which way up their Pantacles should be". This was a reference to the inevitable bickering among different factions of occultists which occurs still today. Part of the idea of modern Chaos Magic is that all methods are correct, one tradition as valid as another so long as it gets results. The IOT was described in the ad as "readying itself to spread the gnosis", the methods described as "not dependent on any symbolic system or mystification...they are the root techniques powering all systems." The advert also went on to say that the IOT was not an artificial hierarchy, which is one of the main points that separate the IOT from other magical Orders. The intention was that degrees would indicate attainment rather than authority, and that leaders and authority figures would not exist beyond the bare minimum needed to organize things.

Liber Null was drawing more attention than the ad itself at this time, and human nature being what it is, the ideal of non-hierarchy was already somewhat compromised by the inclination of people to see Peter Carroll as the leading figure in the IOT. There were some experiments in collective work with this early group, but it was not long before Ray Sherwin dropped out of the IOT and Peter Carroll went on to officially form "The Pact of the Illuminates of Thanateros", or simply "The Pact". Sherwin and Carroll remained friends and Sherwin is still involved in Chaos Magic in England, although not directly with the IOT.

In the early 1980's, a copy of *Liber Null* appeared in Germany. There was no copyright or address for the author, so a magician and writer, known to the public today as Frater U.D. translated it to the German language. Frater U.D. was a teacher of practical magick, and it was inevitable that he and Peter Carroll would meet. Frater U.D. was initiated into The Pact and given a grade appropriate to his experience. He celebrated his first Chaos-Mass with Carroll in 1985.

This was only the beginning of the proliferation of the IOT. In the mid-1980's The Pact had become an international organization including temples in England, Germany, Austria, Switzerland and Australia. An annual meeting at a castle in Austria became a traditional setting for the international factions to meet and share ideas about magic, which continues to this day.

The magazine, *Chaos International* appeared in 1986 and became associated with the IOT, although articles and opinions were certainly not limited to Pact members. The original idea of this magazine was that editorship would change with each issue and that the magazine would represent all Chaos Magicians and groups following this current. The first two issues were edited by P. D. Brown and Ray Sherwin, then the editorship passed through the hands of a few others before settling in the capable hands of Ian Read, who has done an excellent job with it ever since. Other magazines focusing on the subject of the chaos current have come and gone, but *Chaos International* has continued on and its popularity has spread to other countries. Part of the reason for this is the lack of bias for particular ideas although the magazine is still associated with The Pact, it still represents the freedom of thought and ideas indicative of all Chaos Magicians.

In 1988 it was decided that Lola Babalon, a European member who had been living in California for two years, would start an IOT temple in the U.S.A. She had studied magic with Frater U.D. and had attained the 3rd degree required to start a temple. This temple was eventually dissolved when Lola resigned from the IOT for personal reasons, and other temples in Southern California now represent the American faction of the IOT. Lola has remained active in the magical community and is involved with another new magical group in Southern California.

In an announcement in *Chaos International #12*, Peter Carroll announced his formal retirement as the head of the IOT. Carroll stated that he had decided to spend more time on his family and business. He also stated that he leaves the organization in good hands, although he does not name his successor. One may speculate that this is because the occult climate in England had been a bit strained at the time due to the pirating and showing of a film with reported occult overtones on British television which had given fuel to the fire of religious fanaticism against all people and organizations related to any form of new age or occult activity, but I must emphasize that this is only speculation. He mentions that he may continue to write "articles and the occasional book."

The history of the IOT looked at as a whole is fascinating. The organization is modern, yet quite serious. The rapid spread of IOT temples to several countries and its endurance indicate not only an appeal to contemporary magic users, but also a synchronicity with the times in which it has grown up.

There are other groups and individuals who practice some form of Chaos Magic, yet the IOT has become so well known as to be looked upon as a central (dis) organizational force. History will likely show its importance along with other well known magical organizations, but with a special emphasis on revolution-ary ideas and open-mindedness for new methods and ideas uncommon to magical groups in the past. It will be interesting to observe the unfolding of this history as it continues into the coming years.

In some areas, new Chaos groups have been formed by ex-IOT members who have left the Order for whatever reasons. This is especially prevalent in America where the cultural influences are not as conducive to the original non-hierarchical intent of the founders of the Order. One could almost visualize the spreading of Chaos in a fractal pattern of self-similarity through the proliferation of these splinter groups.

Chaos is also making itself apparent in the workings of other academic magical groups. The writings of A O Spare, Kenneth Grant, Ray Sherwin, Ramsey Dukes, Peter Carroll, and others of recent popularity have become basic textbook information among ceremonial magicians just as the writings of Dion Fortune, the Farrars, and others are classics to the Wiccan communities. Articles relating to Chaos Magic appear with increasing frequency in mainstream new age magazines. There are still only a few books on the market dealing directly with Chaos, partially because good books on the subject are still often privately published in limited editions.

Chaos Magic is a return to basic magical principles, yet it is seen as an advanced level of magical knowledge because one must learn about all the trappings of illusion and deception in 'systems' of magic before the basics can be seen for what they are. In ritual we 'deceive' ourselves into a belief which can then become reality. A. O. Spare had much to say about the role which belief, or suspension of it, plays in ritual. The art of looking beyond what we simply accept as true to alternate possibilities plays a part in science as well as magic. Many of the basic principles of how things work in magic are beginning to find some explanations in an area of science which has only recently begun to gain respectability. It has been very appropriately dubbed, "chaos science".

Chaos Science

Chaos science is an area still not entirely accepted by mainstream science, yet it is something which is not likely to go away despite the discomfort it creates for the status quo. There are several good books in print on the subject of chaos science, yet these are written by scientists who invariably explain the subject in their own familiar terms, which those of us who did not major in physics or math may have a little trouble keeping up with.

It is my purpose in this chapter to explain the various elements of chaos science, including just a little history, to the average reasonably intelligent person who is not familiar with the language of scientists and may even shy away from physics math. The need for this became apparent to me some time ago when I first began investigating the subject myself. There were a lot of people who asked me to explain this subject to them, despite the fact that I make no secret of the fact that I lack a science degree myself. The last straw was when a friend of mine, who is a well-educated, published writer and who teaches Latin and Greek, came to me for an explanation admitting to being bewildered by the same books that I use for reference.

If the reader holds a science or mathematics degree, and is looking for detailed information on this subject or instructions for programming a computer to draw fractal patterns, I recommend that s/he refer to one of the books written solely on the chosen area and leave this chapter to us common folk.

The Meaning of Chaos

Many creation myths begin with a point called chaos from whence comes all matter. Chaos can be represented as a calm center of non-creation or as a tumultuous ocean of possibilities, but the concept of being the beginning and end of all things is almost universal among the known mythologies of the world.

The chaos scientists are attempting, among other things, to explain the nature of creation from infinite potential in their studies on the workings of nature. It is an area where mathematicians, physicists, biologists, chemists, and even meteorologists have had to learn to communicate with one another in order to recognize the similarity of the natural laws governing the behaviour of a wide variety of systems in the real world. In their own scientific way, they look for a cause for things where apparently acausal effects have occurred.

Chaos science studies the connections between different types of irregularity in our world. It tackles the problem of the nature of disorder which scientists have habitually avoided for many years. It seems likely that eventually they will be able to explain it all to us in great detail and become respected among their peers for all their trouble, but for now the science is still considered new and somewhat suspect. Even the generally accepted sciences of psychology and hypnosis are still considered somewhat dubious in some quarters. New areas of science have traditionally gone through a period of resistance before being slowly accepted into the mainstream of accepted theory. Chaos theory will come into its own in time.

Chaos science is largely a study of self-similar patterns in nature and natural phenomena. These patterns, often referred to as "chaotic" or "random", include studies of such areas as the cause of turbulence in fluids, the patterns of coastlines or cloud formations, cyclic patterns in such things as the rise and fall of species populations and the self-similar patterns of the growth of living things. All of these things fall under the heading of chaos science. Certain terms and phrases have become part of the language of chaos science. Among them are; The butterfly effect, fractal, strange attractor and the Mandelbrot set.

It is becoming clear through the study of irregularity and unpredictability that in the real world, the laws of order and chaos are intertwined, each giving rise to the other. The strange laws behind chaotic phenomena hold explanations for the things which we find remarkable in our world, from such physical oddities as the pattern of the human heartbeat, the irregularity of a coastline and the path of a forest fire, to the nature of creative thought in the human mind, and even creation itself. It has been observed that very ordered systems will fall apart in nature, such as the human heartbeat which is naturally aperiodic. On the other hand, apparently chaotic systems will give rise to order.

Scientific reductionism imagines that everything in nature can be disassembled and reassembled into component parts, such as molecules, atoms, electrons, etc., and that at some point we could discover the very smallest of basic particles which would allow us to understand all that there is to know about the universe and everything in it. The reductionists of the nineteenth century dismissed chaotic systems as randomness, or as passive entropy, which is a term referring to the progressive disorganization of useful energy in a system.

Any machine in operation turns some of the energy into a form which cannot be recovered and used again, therefore requiring an energy source to fuel it. This was maddening to the nineteenth century scientists who theorized that through Newtonian laws, it should be possible to invent a perpetual motion machine. This is a demonstration of a dissipative structure. Dissipation suggests something which falls apart, as opposed to structure. A dissipative structure is a system which is capable of maintaining its identity only if it remains open to the flux and flow of its environment. It is a creature of a non-linear world, which is an area which didn't attract very much scientific interest at the time.

To understand what constitutes the scientific study of chaos, it is helpful to explain the meanings of some of the terms and phrases which have become part of the language of chaos.

The Butterfly Effect

"The Butterfly Effect" is a name given to a phenomenon which is more technically referred to as "sensitive dependence on initial conditions". This idea was first modelled on a computer graph by Edward Lorenz, an MIT meteorologist who had a fascination for the way patterns in the atmosphere changed over time, keeping within statistical averages yet never exactly repeating themselves.

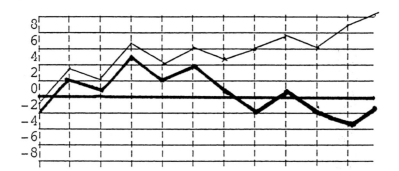

The Butterfly Effect

A standard weather forecast chart or any similar prediction chart can
approximate a result from initial conditions, but a minute fluctuation
in data can have dramatic effects. The chart above represents the
result of a slight variation in initial data entered into a computer, run
(dark line), then repeated with two additional decimal places for the
second run (thin line).

In 1960, he had been working on feeding non-linear equations into a computer to try to model the Earth's atmosphere. He repeated a weather forecast, rounding off the figures in the equations to three decimal places rather than the six decimal places used in the first run. A scientist would expect to find similar results from the two tests, with only a slight variation caused by the tiny inaccuracy.

What actually appeared on the graphs resulting from this test was a shocking revelation. At first the typical graphic pattern of rises and dips above a central line followed a similar pattern, with the expected slight variation for inaccuracy, then suddenly the pattern split into two entirely different patterns, completely unrelated to one another. The combination of non-linearity and iteration had magnified the microscopic difference in the equations in the two computer runs, indicating that a very slight variable in the initial conditions of the test resulted in an entirely different outcome. This was compared within the context of weather patterns to the example of the microscopic effects of a butterfly flapping its wings in Hong Kong, which could set up a change in air currents, magnified progressively through currents in the atmosphere until it resulted in a rainstorm in New York. Thus the term, "butterfly effect".

In a non-linear equation used to model a system in nature, a very small variable can have an extreme effect. An evolving system which has remained constant for a large range of values can suddenly reach a critical point, where the values split up (referred to as a bifurcation) and the system jumps into an entirely different behaviour, such as turbulence. In the area of natural law, scientists have allowed themselves to believe that given an approximate knowledge of a system's initial conditions, such as a weather pattern or the flow of lava from a volcano, they can calculate the approximate behaviour of the system. Yet these systems can frustrate the researchers by behaving erratically, suddenly moving in a direction completely out of sequence with the predictions. The study of newly recognized laws for these sudden variations in the behaviour of natural phenomena is a major factor in what is now called chaos science.

It has been shown that natural systems follow patterns with certain parameters, but with disturbances. There is an order within disorder in nature, which has only recently, through the studies of Lorenz and a handful of other scientists, been possible to model with computers. What was previously believed to be just random behaviour in natural systems is now shown to be subject to a different set of natural laws than the classical Newtonian laws of deterministic science. This different set of natural laws applies universally to a wide spectrum of different types of irregularity from biological systems to geological formations and even economical patterns. The universality of these laws is the study of chaos science.

Strange Attractor

An attractor is a point within an abstract place referred to as "phase space". Phase space is a term used to describe the dimensions or variables in a system's movement. For example, if one observes the movement of a pendulum swinging back and forth, the trajectory of the pendulum's movement is its phase space. The attractor is the point where the pendulum will eventually come to rest, as a pendulum eventually will if it is left to finish its cycle rather than being pushed or powered by an energy source.

If one gives the pendulum a spin, it will traverse a different pattern of phase space with more dimensions to it, spiralling inward toward the center. But the pendulum will still eventually end up at a fixed point. An attractor is a region or point in a system which exerts a pull on that system. It is a point, like the bottom of a round bowl with a marble set spinning within it, where the system, or marble in this case, will eventually come to rest unless an external forces effects the system, which will start the process again.

These concepts also apply to much more complicated systems, such as ecological systems. In the study of the fluctuations of a species population, it can be observed under controlled conditions that a stable environment with a fixed food supply will support a species population of a specific size. If the species begins to overpopulate, the food supply will be inadequate and the species will decrease to a size which is supported by that food supply. If the method of decreasing the population kills off too large a percentage of that population, the species will breed freely until it reaches the stable level of population. This population level is the attractor in this system.

It is when we begin to notice that the system will vary in periodic patterns that we run into strange attractors. There is a shape within the apparent disorder of chaotic systems. It is a sort of organized disorganization of phase space, which is why chaos scientists call it "strange".

Chaos is not random as it may appear, but a subtle form of order. Computer models of natural phenomena are demonstrated by simply feeding a number between 0 and 1 back into itself, dropping the whole numbers to the left of the decimal point and continuing the process with the fractional values. This results in patterns of numbers which displayed graphically strike an uncanny resemblance to patterns in nature. The diagram of the Lorenz attractor represents a system which is aperiodic- one which almost repeats itself but never quite succeeds.

A strange attractor represents the final state of a dynamic system in a noisy world. The spirals within spirals of Lorenz's diagram represent an orbit in phase space with just a few degrees of freedom. The attractor point follows a path which is nonperiodic, never following the exact same path twice, yet repeating in a similar pattern through the twists and turns of the available phase space.

Turbulence

Turbulence occurs in all sorts of natural phenomena, from weather patterns to eddies in bodies of water, air currents and even supports for bridges, which are not products of nature but are subject to natural laws. Turbulence breaks up orderly systems and causes disorder to interfere with our technology. It is a scaling of disorder. A system of small eddies within larger ones, unstable, and highly dissipative.

Leonardo Da Vinci took an interest in turbulence in flowing water. In his drawings, he noted how vortices tend to fragment into smaller and smaller scales, yet each new subdivided system looking similar to the others. If a river flows rapidly, these systems of eddies within eddies, further subdivided by forming still smaller eddies around obstacles such as rocks, eventually result in turbulence which can manifest very violently as rapids.

In 1948, a German scientist by the name of Eberhard Hopf invented a mathematical model describing the bifurcations leading to turbulence. The subject of the effects of period-doubling in the motion of systems leading to apparently random behaviour of the system is one of the keys to the mysteries of chaos science.

The Mandelbrot Set

Anyone who has done any reading on this subject at all has probably heard the name, Mandelbrot. Benoit Mandelbrot is a mathematician who sometime around 1960 noticed a correlation between theoretical mathematics and patterns in such things as fluctuating cotton prices, or patterns in nature such as population patterns of gypsy moths. His research into real life phenomena which previously seemed entirely random, but could be reproduced into computer graphs, is a major milestone of chaos science.

Mandelbrot, like most of the most well known scientists and mathematicians who have contributed to the science of chaos, had a special talent for intuition about the nature of patterns. Mandelbrot had a strikingly geometrical mind, which could find solutions to mathematical problems through visualizing geometrical diagrams. He could not program a computer, but could 'debug' a program by analyzing the pictures produced by it. The young Mandelbrot cultivated a fascination for the irregularities of geometry in nature while in school, developing an eye for the self-similar patterns in various aspects of nature. He recognized that mountains are not cones, coastlines are not straight.

Mandelbrot is well known for computer images which repeat a given pattern in increasingly smaller dimensions into infinity. These are produced by entering geometrical equations into a computer and watching the process unfold. But there were more than shapes of a classically geometrical nature to discover. Certain equations may draw remarkable likeness of a leaf, or a tree. It became apparent to him that things in nature follow patterns that may seem random, but stay within certain parameters. He saw a system of scaling in nature, where a degree of irregularity will remain constant over different scales. A distant view of a coastline will resemble the same angles as a much closer look at a small part of the same coastline; a distant mountain will have a similar shape to the smaller mounds one may find while climbing the same mountain.

Mandelbrot had discovered the same laws of self-similar attraction which apply to the strange attractor, but was able to demonstrate the creative phenomena graphically through fractal geometry. He worked within fractional dimensions which measured a degree of roughness or irregularity in an object.

Fractal

A fractal image is one with a self-similar pattern. It is created through a process of iteration wherein shapes are repeated in smaller and smaller scales, creating an image which is self-similar to its component parts. Fractals are characterized by infinite detail and infinite length, each component detail being reducible to additional component details into infinity. The word was coined by Mandelbrot himself.

The Latin *fractua*, means irregular, and the adjective *fractus*, from the verb, *frangere*, means "to break". It also holds connotations with words like fractional and fragmented, which relate very closely to the nature of fractal geometry. Fractal equations can be used to

48

demonstrate self-similar patterns in such things as the progressive daily and monthly prices of goods, the cycles of epidemics, or in the clusters of 'noise' during data transmission over a telephone line. They are most apparent in the modelling of natural phenomena, such as the workings of biological systems.

A drawing of the network of blood vessels in the human body is an excellent example. It was determined during Mandelbrot's researches that chaotic patterns are the norm in nature. The human heartbeat, as well as brainwaves, follow a naturally chaotic pattern. A very steady heartbeat with a regular rhythm is known to be a precursor to heart failure. Steady, perfectly rhythmic brainwaves precede an epileptic seizure. Without variation in patterns, we do not live. Yet these variations stay within their specific parameters.

In a phase space diagram of a strange attractor, the movement point of the system folds and refolds in the phase space with infinite complexity. A strange attractor is a fractal curve. Turbulence and disorder in all its forms can be demonstrated through fractal geometry. The same underlying processes which shape mountains, clouds and coastlines are at play in the organic formations of nature such as lungs, the nervous system and blood supplies.

The images created by Mandelbrot's computers are fascinating to watch, as well as aesthetically pleasing to the eye, but observing chaos actually at work in nature, or economic patterns, is far more fascinating. The patterns of smoke rising from a cigarette or milk forming clouds in a cup of tea or coffee takes on a special significance when viewed as a natural manifestation of fractal geometry.

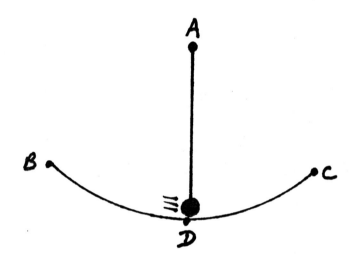

Phase Space is a measurement of the parameters of any given system.
In the simple example above, the movement of the pendulum is
determined by how far it will swing when one end is held in a fixed
position (point A). Phase Space is measured from point B to point C,
and the attractor is at point D where gravity will eventually cause the
pendulum to stop.

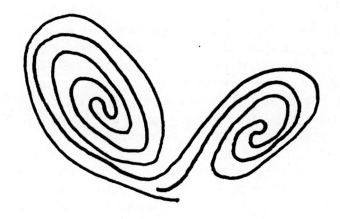

Lorenz Attractor

The above diagram represents a typical example of the design made
against a graph of one of Lorenz's equations. The latered, intertwining
spiral and double sapiral designs created from these graphs bring to
mind the labyrinth designs found on many ancient monuments (see
diagram in Chapter 5).

The branches of a tree are a clear demonstration of fractals in nature. The large branches divide into smaller and smaller branches, down to the level of twigs. The root system of the same tree will mirror this branching process through the soil. The branching angles will be preserved throughout the reducing scales. Fractal modellers can use this method to produce computer images of trees or other organic forms by entering different numbers for each different species. Leonardo Da Vinci made the observation that the thickness of a tree trunk will equal the thickness of the collective branches above any given point along the system. This fractal structure also makes it possible for each branch to support the weight of the subsequent branches, as well as the stresses of wildlife and weather. The beams and trusses and girders of the Eiffel Tower branch into a lattice of ever-thinner members which allows the structure strength with minimal weight.

The human circulatory system is another example of fractal geometry at work. The volume of blood comprises only three percent of the body. Within the constraints of the body are two intertwining systems, one for delivery of oxygen and the other for the elimination of waste products, each of which must come from a central pumping system and branch out into a system of smaller and smaller pipes in such a way that no part of tissue is very far from the system. The heartbeat itself follows a fractal rhythm. Each beat is similar to the last, but never quite the same. Disruption of this fractal rhythm can result in congestive heart failure if the rate becomes too regular, or in the defibrillation of a heart attack if it becomes too aperiodic. Fractals work in a fractional dimension between periodicity and aperiodicity.

Causality

Linear causality can work in an isolated laboratory situation, but in the real world there is no way to shield an entity from effects of various phenomena. Any number of subtle factors affect everything in the universe at any given time. For example, if one hits a tennis ball over a net, it seems that it would be at least theoretically possible to calculate the exact trajectory of the ball if the initial conditions are known, which would include the amount of force exerted on the ball, the density of the atmosphere, and the exact position on the ball where the tennis racket will strike. However, this trajectory will also be affected by small wind currents and forces of gravity from the Earth and any bodies which may affect it. An insect colliding with the ball may cause a minute variation in speed and exact trajectory, which could escalate into a totally different result than the initial conditions may have indicated. Newtonian laws of causality can be very useful in describing mechanistic systems, but the natural world quite often requires a totally different approach.

Linear systems can be very predictable up to a certain point, often referred to by chaos scientists as the "critical point", where turbulence manifests. To accelerate an automobile one pushes on a pedal, which increases the fuel input and results in a smooth acceleration of speed. However, if one accelerates beyond a certain point, the car will begin to vibrate violently or the engine may overheat and freeze up. If one applies heat to a container of water, the warmer water will rise to the surface resulting in convection, commonly known as a "rolling boil".

Non-linear dynamical systems, whether chaotic or stable, are so complex they are unpredictable in their detail. A clock or a robot operates by simple deterministic principles which are easy to explain by a few simple laws and to reproduce. The mind, on the other hand, operates with a subtlety and speed which is apparently of an entirely different order. The pancreas secretes fluids to aid in the digestion of food, but the brain secretes consciousness. In Cartesian duality, mind and matter are both treated as substances. Matter is the substance which can be held in the hand, while mind is the invisible, intangible substance. The world has been found to contain invisible energy fields and elementary particles which do not have paths or properties which can be properly determined in the absence of an observer.

If two or more people engage in conversation, there is a flow of active meaning between or among them. This meaning will cause subtle transformations within the brain of each participant, in turn effecting the thought and action of each of the individuals. The brain constantly reacts to the background of information in the external environment, in turn acting back on the environment and forming a new perspective of reality. This is a constant process of change which reflects outward into the person's experience of society, human relationships, self image and also on the physical world through action.

An example of human behaviour which demonstrates the bifurcation feedback which is typical of the laws modelled by diagrams of the strange attractor, is communication networking. Communication networks exist in many forms which include personal contact, postal correspondence and computer bulletin boards. The computer bulletin boards, commonly referred to as bbs's, are an excellent example of this phenomena as they consist of an artificial hierarchy of systems operators (called sysops) and a large subordinate network of users. The central computer itself represents the attractor in each system. Each of the sysops runs a service where individual users call in on their computer modems and exchange information or messages with other users of the system. The example could get very complicated if we try to carry it through to the relationships of different systems which communicate with each other, in some cases forming large interdependent systems of worldwide communication among large numbers of people who share a common interest, so let's keep it simple and deal with a single central computer which attracts a number of users, who call in to the system.

The system has limited parameters in that there are only so many hours in the day, and only one user can operate over a single telephone line at any given time. A system may have more than one telephone line, but there will still be a finite number of computer hours available which is simple to calculate by multiplying the number of lines by the number of hours in which the system operates. Of course there will be periods where nobody calls into the system, which will vary with the circumstances of the collective users and create a non-periodic system of computer hour parameters within the system of users.

Over a period of time, it can be seen that a certain number of users will appear sporadically, sometimes only a few times over a short period of time before they disappear, presumably because for whatever reason they have lost interest in that particular system. Patterns form of the number of frequent users who exist at any given time, as 'regulars' move out of reasonable calling distance or become too busy with other aspects of their lives to sit at the computer terminal to chat as often, while other new participants appear, some of which will become frequent users. This is a network within the larger network, which also includes the variable numbers of occasional or short term users. It would be fascinating to enlist a hard-core computer network junkie to write a program based on chaos mathematics to model the bifurcations of bbs user patterns. The important point is that the results would very likely resemble similar data on species population, or the rise and fall of cotton prices.

Creative Chaos

The noted evolutionary biologist Stephen Jay Gould points out that Darwin's Origin of Species was interpreted very differently by Russian intellectual Petr Kropotkin than the way it was interpreted by European and American scientists. Kropotkin found in nature a system of cooperation rather than competition. Eminent biologists such as Gould have pointed out that research does not support the neo-Darwinian view that gradual accumulation of mutations will eventually lead to new species.

Researchers have bombarded the DNA of fruit flies with X-rays and other treatments to cause mutations, which has led to all sorts of variations and monstrosities, yet none of these mutations was sufficient to create a new species of fly. Skeletons in rock indicate new species which appear with relative suddenness rather than as a result of accumulated variations. The evolutionary change in DNA allows a species to adapt to its environment but does not change the genetic blueprint of the species. Evidence shows that species survive by adapting to changes in the environment. The species itself will maintain its 'blueprint' through these adaptations. If it cannot adapt, it will die. This ability to adapt to change in the environment could be similarly modelled for the creative process of the human mind.

A mind that is constantly sensitive to change is in tune with the natural order of synchronicity. Natural creativity pervades every element of nature, yet is not apparent to a large extent in the life of the average person. Those who demonstrate seemingly unlimited creativity are considered to be specially gifted. Most people, caught up in the daily routines of jobs, families and relationships perceive their creativity as very limited. Time and energy are expended on these daily occurrences to the exclusion of creative effort. The blame for their lack of creativity is often put down to circumstances.

Chaos science may well hold the secret of human imagination. One of the common factors among the mathematicians and scientists who have contributed to the study of chaos is intuition. Most scientists will admit that the mind is capable of affecting our own bodies in ways which are beyond current understanding. A few may even admit that there is evidence that mind can affect environment, in both subtle and less subtle ways. This is where chaos begins to relate to magic, because the same patterns in nature which have been modelled on the computers of chaos scientists also apply to the patterns inherent in magic.

Patterns of Chaos

People who practice magic, and many people who don't, will sometimes observe that things which happen in their lives seem to fall into patterns. An unusual, or even sometimes bizarre, set of circumstances may occur to make it easy, or even compulsory, to meet a particular person or be in a particular place at a time when something significant is going to happen. An equally bizarre set of circumstances may prevent one from doing something which was intended, and in some cases a reason why it should have been avoided will be discovered later.

Karl Jung coined the term "synchronicity" to describe situations here apparently acausal events seem to relate to one another. Most people experience at some time or another something which may be seen as coincidence. Perhaps one thinks of an old friend for the first time in many years, and then receives a telephone call from that friend or 'accidentally' comes across the person while walking in an area where one wouldn't have thought to run across that particular person.

One of the classic examples is from Jung's own experience of a gold-green scarab beetle landing on the window sill of his office while listening to a patient relate a dream about a golden scarab. There are many examples of these odd coincidences, some more difficult to explain away than others. Scientists mostly dismiss them as "just coincidence", but some of us experience them on such a regular basis that it becomes a pattern in our lives. In some cases we begin to expect them, or perhaps even look to magic as a way of encouraging them to happen.

Some patterns are more subtle; a series of occurrences over a long period of time will lead one down a particular path in life. It has been said that someone who reaches an advanced age can look back over their life and see how events seem to fit together like chapters in a story which has been well plotted, rather than a random series of events.

In the case of someone who accomplishes great things after starting out life in difficult circumstances, this long pattern can show all sorts of "coincidences" which somehow fit together, giving the person opportunities which may not have been available to another person. It can be seen where certain events would have to have happened, despite being very unlikely, for the person to have reached their state of achievement.

It is not uncommon to learn that such an achiever has been led by their own drive and initiative to a large degree, and the hardcore empiricist will not hesitate to point out that with that drive, the person in question will, to a large extent, create their own opportunities. However, if one follows the entire history of the person's road to success, there will certainly be opportunities which have appeared 'accidentally', in a way that cannot be explained through the actions of the achiever or their supporters. Again, the empiricist will shout "Coincidence! Pure chance!" The magician will, on the other hand, recognize that the

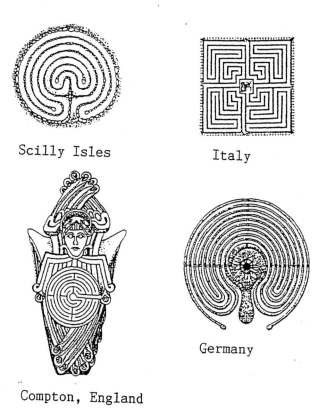

Scilly Isles

Italy

Compton, England

Germany

Labyrinths

Many ancient sites have labyrinth designs carved into monuments or structures across the globe. The similarity of these designs arising from widely varying cultures and locations is a source of much archaeological speculation.

achiever's state of mind, affected by determination and confidence, will have influenced what is now commonly referred to as the "probability factor".

A good friend of mine, who happens to be an English Wiccan, explained to me that he and many others of his particular tradition are quite happy to simply observe these patterns of life without making any attempt to understand how or why they happen. He goes on to explain that part of their belief system includes accepting the mysteries of life simply as mysteries. They believe in keeping the wonder of it all alive.

I must admit that there is some merit in this attitude. For those who practice magic most often in a religious context, mainly for celebratory or healing rituals, there really is no reason to dissect mysticism into component parts, upsetting the probability factor with an overload of deterministic facts. There is no merit to draining away the spiritual nature of magic until it becomes no more than another reductionist scientific explanation for the workings of nature. However, none of us are likely to actually accomplish this dissection however hard we try, simply because magic does not lend itself to linear Newtonian physics any more than the world of creative nature does in reality, as is being observed in the study of chaos science.

Those of us whose lives are directly affected by our individual magical operations (in that we perform rituals to affect elements of our daily activities) seek to understand, as best we can, the nature of patterns in a magical universe because we have the events of our lives shaped by our magical workings.

Understanding how these patterns are affected by our actions, our rituals, and even the forming of an intent in our minds, becomes a matter of exercising control over the way in which our lives will unfold.

This brings us back to the term, "probability factor". It is an obvious term, describing the level of probability of success in any magical operation. This is where understanding the art of making coincidences happen begins. We start with an intent. There is something we want to happen.

A classic example is a desire for more money. There are several approaches one might take to accomplishing this, depending on the beginning circumstances. The probability factor relates how likely it is that the goal will be accomplished through the method which will be tried. For example, if a person wants to win money through a lottery or any random contest, the odds of winning are going to be well stacked against him/her in the initial conditions. If this is a working person, attempting to conjure up a better job, a pay rise, or circumstances which will lead to starting a business each have their own probability factor, all of them more likely than the contest.

To apply magic to any of these methods of achieving the goal has the potential of tipping the odds, but there is a much higher probability factor that our subject will find a better job or get a rise than win the lottery. That doesn't mean it would hurt to buy a lottery ticket, but filling out a few applications or talking to the boss about a pay rise would be a good idea to go along with whatever magical operation is performed.

Most often, money rituals will result in smaller windfalls which "just happen to" cover a specific need, rather than result in large fortunes for no particular purpose other than idle greed.

Just like the patterns depicted by diagrams of strange attractors in chaos science, patterns in life and magic fall within parameters and expanding beyond the parameters of natural phenomena is more difficult, and more risky, than influencing a path within those parameters. by changing our state of mind, we can change the patterns of events in our lives and to a reasonable extent control our destinies.

There is a dual nature to this area of magic. On the one hand, controlling our destinies has the advantage of leading us toward our goals. On the other hand, we must remember that the mysteries are still there for us. There will always be factors at work which we know nothing about. To try to force events to follow a particular pattern can prevent us from recognizing another pattern which is attempting to unfold naturally. We can do ourselves a disservice in exerting too much control.

For example, if our above subject should get stuck into the idea that the only way to accomplish the goal is to find a different job, and performs a ritual toward this end as well as making full effort to look for the new position, there is a risk that another opportunity, such as a promotion on the horizon, will be overlooked and the old job may be quit just before the promotion would have been bestowed. If our imaginary friend had kept his mind open to all possibilities, he may have gone through the motions of looking for a new job, but kept the old one while waiting for a pattern to manifest, keeping all senses alert for subtle changes in events. Whether he would have been happier with the promotion or the new job elsewhere is another story altogether.

Magic in Thought and Deed

Probability and consequences are things which it is wise to keep in mind when performing any act of magic. An act of magic can be anything from a full blown psychodrama ritual to an intent formed in the mind, even a stray thought in some cases. It is the subtle transformation of mental energy, one might say thought projection, which begins the process of change in the environmental conditions affected by that thought, leading to a different series of events than may have happened had the intent never occurred. This is a subtle, but very effective, form of magic which is well illustrated by the example of the "butterfly effect" in the section of this book on chaos science.

The effects that a person's state of mind can have on his/her immediate environment cannot be weighed or measured by scientists except in the case of psychological changes which actually change the behaviour of the person in question. That a person's thoughts can change events surrounding him/her outside of the sphere of direct actions is an apparently acausal result, yet it happens repeatedly, frequently and often.

Current science cannot explain how or why this occurs, although there are theorists among the chaos scientists who have recognized the fact that it does happen and are giving it some degree of study. The magician studies not so much how it happens, as how to make it happen. Much of what is experienced in ritual or other application of magical operation is very difficult to describe to someone who has not had that experience. Much of what occurs is sensed in what I can only call a psychic manner, yet on an emotional level, rather than seen or heard in a mental way. To form an intent in one's mind, and simply know that the purpose is already achieved by that formation of thought, is an experience that I have spent much of my life trying to explain to myself and others with whom I have studied some form of magic or other. It was this quest which eventually led me to the study of chaos theory.

Quite a lot has been written, especially since the 1960's, about the 'energy' or 'substance' of magic. Basic magic books will explain the four basic alchemical elements, earth, air, fire and water, and then go on to try to explain the fifth element, aether. Some people refer to it as spirit, but I find that term not quite appropriate.

Aether is described as the substance through which magical 'energy' travels, or the fabric of space/time. This is an attempt to explain something which is not really energy, yet is something we do not have another term handy to describe. It is a concept which must be understood in its own terms. The early alchemists brought forth the word 'aether' to describe the medium in which magical operations are manifest. The 'substance' of aether is affected by thought or intent, much as air currents are affected (theoretically at least) by the flapping of a butterfly's wings as illustrated by the 'butterfly effect'. The purpose of ritual in magic is to create a mental association with the intent of the magician(s) in the sub-conscious minds(s), which in turn creates a change in the aetheric fabric, and therefore causes change of some kind to occur.

Creative Chaos is the creative principle behind all magic. When a magical ritual is performed, regardless of 'tradition' or other variables in the elements of performance, a virtual magical 'energy' is created and put into motion to cause something to happen. One could say that all magical 'energy' is chaos 'energy' because once a magical operation is performed, the 'energy' is out of the hands of the magician and the result will depend on many factors. These include the amount of control the magician was able to exercise during the operation, which in turn depends on experience and ability as well as outside influences.

The word 'energy' used in this context is perhaps not the best choice of terms as I have already said, but what I am attempting to describe is somewhat hindered by the finite limitations of language. Repeating myself again, in the spirit of the 'butterfly effect', a successful magical operation creates a change in the 'aetheric substance' which surrounds and permeates all things and results in an apparently acausal effect.

The trick is to learn not only how to make your magical operations work at all, but also to have some reasonable control over the eventual effect. Magic is a subtle force, just as is chaos in nature, and is subject to variables of all kinds. This is one of the reasons why magic has been regarded as dangerous by many religions, apart from outright prejudice, and why spiritual leaders through history have often attempted to keep it for the 'priestly caste' of whatever culture to which they belonged.

This hasn't always kept the common folk from practising their own 'small magics', although the 'official' attitude runs from outright suppression to shrugging it all off as local superstition. Never mind that Bessy the cow really did start giving milk again after her mistress performed some backwoods ritual having to do with cat bones and sawdust.

Patterns of Chaos

Anyone who has studied Earth energies in the forms of 'ley lines', 'cup and ring markings' on standing stones, etc., is familiar with the spiral patterns depicted on ancient monuments and in landscape designs such as the labyrinths common to earth mounds in Great Britain, as well as many other places in the world. In studying strange attractors in chaos science we find similar spiral patterns in the computer images which represent the patterns of natural phenomena.

The noticeable similarity between a computer image of a path followed around a strange attractor and an Earth mound labyrinth, is in the manner in which the inner-folding pathways twist within themselves, covering every bit of space within a constricted area, yet the paths never cross. Scientists and archaeologists have been speculating on the purpose of Earth mysteries such as labyrinths and standing stones for many years. Some validity can be found for many different theories, the most widely accepted in the case of circles of standing stones is that they were used for astronomical observation.

While this theory seems to fit well with the positioning of stones erected into circles, it does not explain the individual stones found in a wide variety of locations across the British countryside. Some of the stones have been credited as marking stones for old Roman roads, yet others are found in fields or other out of the way locations. These stones are often believed by the local populations (sometimes just as an old superstition in modern times) to have healing properties. People have reported feeling a "tingling" sensation when they touch certain stones, and in some cases a violent rocking sensation, although companions observing the person touching the stone detect no actual movement either from the stone or the person touching it.

In the book *Earth Magic* by Francis Hitching (William Morrow & Co., New York, 1977.), there is mention of an experiment carried out on a twelve-foot-high standing stone in Crickhowell in South Wales, which had been reported by Bill Lewis, a Welsh water diviner, to emit a force which he could sense. Lewis said that the force periodically waxed and waned, and he wished to try to find out if this could be scientifically demonstrated.

A professor of mathematics at King's College in London, John Taylor, who had done some research into paranormal activity provided an instrument called a gaussmeter which is used to measure static magnetic field strength. A young Argentinean physicist, Eduardo Balanovski, went along to make observations. This particular stone was in an unspoiled area where there were many other megalithic cairns, stones, etc. There was no obvious reason for its location, no hilltops, roads, or other indications of a purpose for erecting a stone to mark anything.

Balanovski took some background readings with the gaussmeter, then set it at zero and pointed it at the stone. The results surprised him. The needle shot up to capacity. The results of that day's experiment led to some further study by John Taylor, but the results were unfinished at the time the book was written.

John Williams, a solicitor and dowser who has made a lifetime study of stone monuments, has suggested a link between standing stones and underground water. His theory is that there is a crossing of underground streams beneath each "active" stone. Lewis, who has done work as an electrical engineer, adds that there is experimental evidence which shows that water moving through a tunnel, especially in clay, creates a small static electric field. The crossing of the streams increases the charge, and he believes that the stone placed above the crossing somehow acts as an amplifier. He also suggests that the field emerges from the ground in a spiral pattern of seven bands, two below ground and five above, which changes polarity each month, through a regular cycling process.

This could all be dismissed quite easily, were it not for some of the results of the gaussmeter experiments. The field on the stone was indeed measured in bands, suggesting a spiral. There were also some experiments where Lewis made chalk marks where he felt the bands of force, which were largely confirmed by the gaussmeter readings which recorded double the strength on some of the bands as elsewhere on the stone.

There are many examples to be found of people feeling 'impressions' of some form of energy or force at work in megalithic sites, some well known such as Stonehenge and some only known in their local areas. Williams has said that he feels a representation of positive and negative force in the double spirals at Newgrange.

These experiments were made before research into turbulence and the "critical points" of chaos in nature had become widely known. It would be interesting to see what researchers of chaos science might have to say about experiments with electromagnetic fields connected to megalithic sites, or perhaps even electromagnetic turbulence at underground stream crossings.

An interesting point to keep in mind in view of these experiments is that quartz seems to be a constituent of every "active" stone, and that the molecular structure of quartz is spiral. It is widely accepted among astronomers and physicists now that a spiral force creates the universe itself, as is observable in the spiralling of galaxies. The DNA molecule which is responsible for shaping life is made up in a twin spiral pattern. Some fractal diagrams fall into spiral patterns, although many are more a matter of repeating shapes, but there are quite a lot of these repeating shapes which at some point become spiral or begin to take the shape of waves of some sort.

Where Chaos Dwells

Just as the first chaos scientists were people with an eye for pattern and similarities of form, a Chaos Magician is likely to be a person who can see patterns and similarities in occurrences of everyday life, and therefore can learn to affect the unfolding of a pattern of events. Patterns of various sorts play a large role in magic. Specifically, patterns of events or phenomena are used by magicians as indicators of what to expect to happen in a specific situation, which can then be shaped in accordance with the will of the magician, either through mundane action or magical means. Quite frequently, both will be applied in conjunction.

For example, if our person who was wanting more money were to learn that an opportunity for a promotion existed within his existing workplace, he may see that securing that position could achieve his goal. However, perhaps the position is also coveted by two or three other people, any of which may be qualified to fill it. Our magician would do whatever was mundanely practical to put himself in the running, but would also perform a ritual to give him an 'edge'. This would result in a change in the mindset of the magician, and assuming that the other candidates were not also applying similar means, would result in the magician 'accidentally' coming to the attention of whoever was responsible for making the decision, and eventually being chosen for the position.

If, instead, our magician decided that winning the lottery was the only thing which could satisfy his greed, he would take the mundane action of buying the lottery ticket in conjunction with performing a ritual either in advance, to choose the correct numbers, or after buying the ticket to try to 'will' those numbers to win. The problem he now encounters is that there are many people, some magically inclined and some with other philosophies behind them, who are also in some manner 'willing' their numbers to win. This lowers the probability factor of success for the applied ritual significantly. Any large lottery has many regular players who choose a specific set of numbers time after time, and build up a force of continual 'willing' behind those numbers.

The conflicting wills of many people create a too complicated chaotic mix of influence for any one person to have much of an effect. The idea of a large group of people choosing the same set of numbers and experimenting over a period of time with a combined effort has been discussed from time to time, but I have yet to find a large enough group with the fortitude to see it through over time to try a proper experiment with this.

A more practical lottery experiment for a lone magician would be to follow a particular lottery over time, keeping records of winning numbers very meticulously, and looking for a pattern of repeating numbers over at least a year.

There have been experiments reported in books about chaos science of people attempting to predict the stock market with chaos principles, but with no significant results. The question is, is the experiment a failure, or are the observers unable to properly analyse patterns?

Chaos in Operation

Chaos Magic is not in itself, a system or philosophy. It is rather an attitude that one applies to one's magic and philosophy. A Chaos Magician learns a variety of magical techniques, usually as many as s/he can gain access to, but sees beyond the systems and dogmas to the concepts of physics behind the magical force and will use whatever methods are appealing or effective for him/herself.

Chaos magic does not come with a specific Grimoire or even a prescribed set of ethics. For this reason, it is sometimes dubbed as "left hand path" by some who choose not to understand that which is beyond their own chosen path. There is no set of specific spells which are considered to be 'Chaos Magic spells', although there are a growing number of 'magical workings' which are becoming commonly practised in some Chaos Magic groups. These are simply a matter of choices made by those people who have chosen to become members of those groups.

A Chaos Magician will use the same spells as those of other magical paths, or those of his/her own making. Any and all methods and information are valid, the only requirement is that it works. Mastering the role of the sub-conscious mind in magical operations is the crux of it, and the state called "vacuity" by Austin Osman Spare is the road to that end.

Anyone who has participated in a successful ritual has experienced the 'high' which this state induces. This is not a 'high' from any artificial substance, but one which is induced by the state of mind itself. This state is sometimes referred to as "gnosis" by modern Chaos Magicians.

Experience in magical ritual and results is the way to the understanding of this state of mind. It is similar to the euphoric state which has been induced by many religious practices in the history of the human race by a variety of methods, such as the spinning of Muslim dervishes or meditation in many Oriental religions. These methods may be used by Chaos Magicians as well as any number of others to attain the necessary state of mind to perform magic. With experience, it becomes possible to attain that state of mind with little or no preparation, simply by forming an intent in the mind. The adjustment is a subtle one, but is easy to recognize once it has been experienced.

Part of what makes a magician, especially a Chaos Magician, a bit different from other people is simply an awareness of natural laws in a natural world, and an ability to recognize patterns, and subtle changes, within one's own mind as well as in our immediate environment, just as patterns can be observed and influenced in the behaviour of machines, as any computer aficionado can attest to.

A really good car mechanic is one who has an ability to 'tune in' to a car engine, recognizing if something simply doesn't 'feel' right. Shamanic healers have an ability to recognize when a person feels out of balance in some way, some visualizing auras or 'tuning in' to chakra points to influence the balance of energies within a person's body. The magician recognizes patterns of events, and learns to influence them.

Science has not yet learned to measure and control these things, and therefore they fall within the realm of magic. The hardcore empiricist will dismiss that which is not understood as coincidence, or even come up with explanations which are more outlandish than the phenomenon itself, but which can fit into understood scientific parameters, with allowances made for "unknown factors".

Meanwhile, like the proverbial bumblebee who doesn't know that it is aerodynamically impossible for him to fly and therefore goes on flying anyway, the magicians continue to recognize patterns, and to influence those patterns in their own lives through magical practices which are unprovable at present, but continue to work anyway. It is not surprising to observe that people who take an interest in magic in one form or another are to some degree or other very likely to be classified as free thinkers. To question what is considered to be absolute fact can be very risky in some societies, yet there always seem to be some who will question anyway, who may have a propensity for abstract, or non-linear, thinking.

The Non-Linear Mind

We are trained from an early age to think in linear terms, but nature and the chaos within it are non-linear, and therefore require non-linear thinking to be fully understood. Our early schooling directs us in the basic skills of maths and reading, as well as other areas of study such as science which will help us begin to understand our world as we progress. This is a linear system of information presentation which has great value, but it is our non-linear ability for abstract thinking which will make it possible to assimilate the information which is given us and find ways to apply it to the real world.

This sounds simple, yet it requires a shift in the modes of thinking which are encouraged through most school programs. Shifting our thinking process from linear to non-linear, or the reverse, is a natural process when applied to the pattern of typical classroom learning. We are given facts, which are supported by other facts in a linear continuum, then at some level we begin to question the meanings behind the facts or even the validity of the facts themselves, which is a product of non-linear thinking. This can shift us back into a linear mode of investigation into the researches which led to the belief in the original facts. It is when we set out consciously to shift our thinking process between the linear and non-linear that we may find the process more difficult, as we try to understand the process of non-linear thinking in terms of linear research methods.

I once took a logic class in college. Early in the semester, we began learning about syllogisms, which are a very linear form of logic consisting of two premises which prove a conclusion, assuming that the premises are true. For example;

> All cats are quadrupeds.
> Fluffy is a cat.
> Therefore, Fluffy is a quadruped.

This seems very simple, but takes on a whole new dimension when the common structures of everyday language are closely examined for this sort of direct linear logic, as was demonstrated during an assignment in the class. All we had to do was to put paragraphs of everyday language into an equation form which correlated with the above example of premise and conclusion. It sounds simple, and it is once you get the knack.

The equation for the syllogism itself is the simplest of algebraic models. However, pulling the same sort of structure out of a paragraph of actual conversational language, where the premises are subject to all sorts of modifiers, requires a shift in the thinking process. During that lesson, over the space of a week, the class size dropped from 48 to 9 students. The computer programmers were the first to drop out, despite the fact that most of them were taking the class to better understand computer languages.

Those of us who survived that section went on to earn high grades in the class, but more importantly, found that we had achieved a permanent change in our thinking processes. Our lives were changed by that one simple shift of perspective.

By the time the average person reaches the level of university education, the linear thinking process has been deeply imbedded into the mind through years of fact learning and recitation. Analytical thinking is directed to following paths already well trodden such as the reproduction of oft used experiments in science classes. Independent thinking tends to be channelled into parameters of research which are subject to approval.

Thinking in the Non-Linear

Abstract thought is non-linear. Using the imagination is abstract thinking. Everything humankind has ever intended began with an idea for something that did not previously exist. In some cases this was in order to fill a need, in others, it was simply an idea for something of interest to the inventor. Advances in technology is only one example of the results of non-linear, or original thought.

Philosophy is another subject area where there is plenty of room for free-thinking. Ideas of right and wrong, beliefs about the source of life, matters of spirit and the nature of how things work fill volumes of philosophy books, as well as adding insight into many other subjects found on the bookshelf. A real free thinker, however, is not locked into ideas read in books. Books are educational and can open windows to ideas of those who have written them, but they do not teach a person to think independently, even in those rare cases where they encourage the reader to do so.

In that respect, this book is no different. I can encourage my readers to think for themselves, develop their own ideas of magic and the nature of the universe, but there will always be a large part of the population who will read something like this and chant together "yes, yes, we must think for ourselves", like a scene from a Monty Python film, then go on to practice whatever magical methods and philosophy I write into these pages with no thought given to the idea that some percentage of what I write is my own opinion, subject to disagreement.

We are taught from the beginning of our lives to conform to what other people expect us to think and how to behave. Our parents teach us their ideas of religion, politics, and whether or not we should sit in a comfortable position while eating our dinner. As small children we enter school and learn to respond to the sound of a bell, meekly following others of our roboton race into a classroom to have the teacher's ideas spoon fed to us. Eventually we leave school and are expected to fit into a mold of some kind; to be like our parents or other mentors.

Attempts at independent thinking are discouraged at every level of communication with other humans. To disagree with the religious or political positions of our parents is to invite disaster in many cases. To wander very far from accepted theory in our educational institutions can easily result in low grades or unemployment, perhaps loss of funding for research programs. It takes a special form of conviction for a researcher to pursue an idea which is sufficiently far from the mainstream to be considered revolutionary. the early chaos scientists in the 1960's encountered everything from being completely ignored and considered to be eccentrics, to actual opposition to their ideas and attempts to explain them away as "nothing new", even references to significant works which shifted the credit for important breakthroughs to earlier researches of a similar nature.

"Free Belief"

One of the most important elements of Chaos Magic is the ability to suspend or create belief. Austin Spare wrote of his concept of free belief in several of his writings, which is where we get the name. The actual concept is, however, not exclusive to Spare. Many books which 'teach' magic begin with lessons about the importance of imagination in the use of magic, and of actually believing that you can do what you are attempting to do. Many teenagers sit in front of a table after reading these books, straining muscles in their heads while 'willing' a paperclip or some other small object to move across a table.

The idea of free belief is more a matter of suspending belief in a given "known fact". For example, if I try to 'will' rain on a clear day, my belief that the clear sky makes this impossible will prevent me from achieving my goal. However, if I can 'forget' that the sky is clear, and simply expect a cloud to form out of the moisture in the atmosphere, it just might happen. This sort of self-deception takes a bit of practice.

A Chaos Magician will look at the probability of a desired situation, and attempt to suspend belief in the improbability of the desired result. Once the mind is set on the path to the successful result, momentum will generally carry events in the right direction. A Chaos Magician cannot afford to be a pessimist. Although one should not blind oneself to realistic obstacles, the focus should be on surmounting those obstacles rather than giving them power by recognizing them as an opposing force. More often than not, there is a way around obstacles, even though it may require a few 'lucky coincidences'.

Revolutionary Magic

It is really amazing to observe the percentage of our world population who are set in the path of doing things in a particular manner "because we have always done it that way". These people will go to great lengths to impede progress in their sphere of influence, unless it is done in the specific manner which is considered acceptable and conforms to their model of how things should be.

Some of the examples that come to mind are certain individuals who would be considered respectable religious leaders, moralists, scientists, and yes, even magicians.

A great many magicians imagine themselves to be non-conformists to some degree or other. Most of us manage to function in society, in some cases even to the point of outright respectability. Others are inclined to become the rebels of society. In both cases there is a degree of conformity to social norms and acceptable ideas. The 'anarchist' with the spiked hair and pierced flesh who spews forth the finer points of A.O. Spare's magical philosophy is every bit as much conformist as the lawyer in the three-piece-suit who collects the leather bound editions of the same books. They have simply chosen different sectors of society to fit into.

There is no crime in conformity. To a large degree, it is a natural inclination among our species. Society functions as a whole through conformity of individuals to parameters of behaviour. Imagination and creativity can flourish in an atmosphere of reasonable conformity. It is when it goes to the extreme of complacency that the magic of creativity dies. Complacency is the first step on the road to a death in mediocrity. The spirit of chaos is not the same as that of anarchy, or of disorder. To create requires the willingness to wander out of the mold, to be a free thinker and chart new territory. Non-linear thought doesn't lead to rebellion, but frees imagination to create.

The manifestation of that which the imagination creates has been a growing phenomenon for longer than many people realize. It begins with mechanical inventions; someone imagines a tool or machine which does not exist and then creates it from raw materials. This has been happening at a very rapid rate over the last 200 years. We are past that stage into a more spiritual realm of invention now. Technology keeps creating new possibilities on the physical plane, meanwhile, we are only now beginning to truly understand the workings of real magic. Those who worship the magicians of the past, as opposed to the philosophers, blind themselves to the true nature of magical possibilities. Magic is not method so much as intent. To understand the workings of magic transcends the methods used by others. A Chaos Magician understands that whatever methods are used are no more than an outward display of an inner transformation.

The alchemists of the past pursued inner transformation, yet wrote of the transmutation of metals. There is rumour that in some cases, there may have been alchemists who could actually accomplish these metalurgic transmutations, but more often it is learned that someone who attempted these experiments was injured as a result of an explosion. Some believe that the alchemist's writings were meant to be symbolic of the quest to transmute the soul into purity.

Chaos Magicians seek to harness the power of the subconscious mind to perform magic. They understand the concept that whatever symbols we use, whether god forms or traditional correspondences or something else, they are only symbols for our minds like the symbols which our minds present to us in dreams. They may not see any point in purifying the soul like an alchemist, or exclusively performing healing rituals as some of the pagan religions are inclined to.

There are many chaos magicians who join groups and subsequently fall into the inevitable habit of performing rituals with a similar formula as is practised by the rest of the group. This is an unavoidable factor in group workings, as synchronization of the members is necessary to perform a ritual at all. Still, the true freethinkers realize that they do not have to always practice as part of the group. They do not always have to share the ideas and ethics of the group. They are free to develop methods and ideas of their own.

True freedom is a frightening thing to mainstream society. In the film, *Easy Rider*, Jack Nicholson gives a wonderful speech to Peter Fonda and Dennis Hopper about the nature of freedom in society. The 1960's film is set mostly in Texas, a part of the American south where conformist groups like the KKK are known to still exist.

Two motorcyclists (Fonda and Hopper) are travelling across the state toward Louisiana for Mardi Gras. They are camped out with their temporary travelling partner (Nicholson), who they met in jail after being arrested for parading without a permit; the result of goodnaturedly joining a small town parade on their motorcycles. Nicholson explains to them that the small town people fear them because they represent a level of freedom that they themselves are afraid of. They are refused service in a restaurant because of their appearance and the motorcycles which represent the freedom to live outside of the formula of job, family and church which is the accepted mode of life among the local citizens. The point is driven home when the character played by Nicholson is beaten to death during the night by a mob of these 'good citizens'.

It is this sort of hypocrisy which the Chaos Magician seeks to avoid by freeing the mind to examine the question of ethics for oneself. A Chaos Magician may examine the old parameters of what is acceptable or not within the use of magic. An old formula which was popular to quote a few decades ago was that magic used for healing was white magic, while magic used for selfish ends was black magic, and therefore evil.

I do not know who started this formula, but who is this person to define evil for me? If I heal myself, is that then evil? If I want to perform a ritual to improve my financial position, is that black magic? And why should black magic be equated with evil in the first place? Chaos Magicians do not shy away from using magic for selfish ends, or from using methods which may be frowned upon by religious pagans.

The Darkside of Chaos

"Do not hide from darkness. Only in balance is truth to be found." --Nick Frost

Chaos Magicians are sometimes dubbed, "left hand path", which is mostly a result of openly using magic as we see fit rather than limiting ourselves to healing rituals. This labelling phenomenon is generally taken with good humour, and sometimes even encouraged as the free-thinkers among us tend to see the humour in allowing the ignorant to fear what they do not choose to examine.

The general term, "darksider", has recently come into common use for nearly any category of occultist who isn't specifically Wiccan or a member of a traditional ceremonial group. This term can have a double meaning though. Chaos Magicians are likely to be more aware of their own dark side than the average person. Recognizing the part of ourselves that isn't all white light and rainbows is considered to be a survival tool against the possibility of our own fears and imperfections rising from the subconscious in mid-ritual to confront us. Darkness also represents mystery; the unknown territory. The Chaos Magician looks into the unknown, tries new methods and considers all information to be potentially valid. New ideas are not dismissed out of hand because they disagree with accepted facts or opinions. Anything is worth considering and examining.

Chaos Magicians are the revolutionaries of Magic, the explorers into the mechanics behind the entire spectrum of ritual methods to learn for themselves just what makes them work, or not.

Names of Chaos:
gods and other creatures

Chaos Magicians are not required by any 'central creed' to believe or practice with any specific gods or pantheon. Free belief plays a major role in the chaos mentality, and the choice of whether or not to believe in anything at all outside of oneself lies entirely with the individual magician, and can change with the individual in accordance with need and circumstance. In fact, most Chaos Magicians recognize that god-forms are simply symbols to our subconscious and that we create our own gods, and daemons, to fill our symbolic needs. With that said, it is also true that there are a few specific god-forms, chosen out of historic mythologies and in some cases even fiction novels, which have become popular symbols among Chaos Magicians.

The odd thing is that these god-forms seem to take on a life of their own and behave in a similar fashion to different magicians who 'call' or 'invoke' them in ritual. This is not an unusual phenomenon historically, yet it does bring a lot of philosophical consideration to the nature of 'thought form entities' and other apparently external beings.

The qualities of human emotions have been personified by the human race for at least as long as recorded history, quite often in the form of the celestial beings that nearly all of the world's religions worship, frequently known as gods. Different aspects of life, including emotions and day-to-day tasks required for survival, are represented by gods and goddesses who become real, as story characters, to the people who create and worship them. Many of the needs filled by these gods are common to many cultures and although known by different names, the gods and goddesses representing these needs are often very similar in character.

A personification of deity is an identification of thought, patterns of ideas and intent within the human experience. Putting a name on it helps to allow different individuals within a cultural group or through history to experience that particular force in a common manner. To classify it under a title, such as god, daemon or elemental, serves to bring it that much closer to the individual experience.

Personifications of the principle of chaos take many forms, and in historical pantheons often are considered evil, which brings the question to mind of what is behind the concept of good and evil? Most of us accept the explanations of 'what is good' from our parents at a young age, and blindly take the word of our teachers and society of that which constitutes 'evil' as we grow. Those of us who at some point, choose a path of exploration into magic, are often the ones who will question what it is that determines the difference.

When we consider the various gods included in the pantheons we know, we assign these labels of 'good/benevolent' or 'evil/adversary' to most of them. What makes a god or goddess fit into one of these categories?

Why should an 'adversary', such as Satan in the Christian pantheon, be considered evil, rather than just another point of view?

The very name of Satan causes most of us to react in a very fearful and negative way. The archetype of the 'evil' one who will stop at nothing to bring misery to mankind touches our deepest fear response mechanisms, yet how many of us even believe that this entity has any basis in reality? The pre-Christian pantheons also had their gods to fill this role of adversary. The most feared of them were usually those who represented chaos in some form.

As was said in the beginning of this book, the word "chaos" can have several meanings. Often the first to come to mind is that of discord and confusion, and it is our natural fear of confusion and the unknown which has helped to give chaos, and those entities associated with it, such a dubious reputation.

The Greek and Roman pantheons provide an association with this form of chaos in the personification of the goddesses Eris and Discordia respectively. These two have been very closely associated with each other to the point that they are generally considered to be interchangeable, but the most well known story associated with them is actually told about Eris.

Because Eris resented being left off the invitation list at a banquet of the gods in celebration of the marriage to King Peleus and the sea nymph Thetis, she threw into the banquet hall a golden apple with an inscription reading, "For The Fairest". Each of the goddesses wanted to believe that she was the fairest, but the three with the best claim were Aphrodite, Hera and Pallas Athena. They asked Zeus to choose the fairest of them, but he wisely refused and sent them to ask Paris who was tending his father's sheep at Mount Ida, and was considered an excellent judge of beauty.

The story goes on to explain how the goddesses each tried to bribe him to cast his vote for them, and eventually led to the Trojan War when the apple was at last awarded to Aphrodite, who had dropped her garment to reveal her assets.

Often when gods and goddesses are involved, as well as the occasional daemon, the meaning of chaos is likely to turn to creation from the void or Abyss. Most cultures have a creation myth which includes a beginning in the state of primal, unformed chaos. The ruling entity of this unformed state is often conquered in battle by a Sun god of some sort who becomes the great bringer of life and creation, bringing "light into darkness".

Tiamat, who exists in many cultures in the general middle eastern part of the world, is a good example of this. Tiamat is a serpent or dragon goddess, a common symbol of chaos. Her conqueror is the god Marduk. The Babylonian version of Tiamat has her as a composite creature, part animal, part serpent, part bird. She is depicted as evil, and yet as the Universe-Mother who possesses the Tablet of Fate. This is a good example of how the chaotic gods are often depicted as symbols of pre-creation, even as mother figures, and then given connotations of evil after a beginning of time, symbolized by the coming of a Sun God (father figure) who brings life.

One story depicting Tiamat's Universe-Mother attributes, depicts her as goddess of the Primal Abyss, who gives birth to the gods of Mesopotamia. The god Apsu is disturbed by all the noise that these new gods make, and complains about it to Tiamat who has taken the form of a dragon and is living in the sea. She gives birth to lizards, dragons, hurricanes, mad dogs, scorpion-men, fish-men, lion demons and centaurs to use as an army with the renegade god Kingu as their leader to discipline the gods. The frightened gods recruit Marduk as their champion, who uses magic and winds to slay Tiamat and split her in half to form the heavens and earth. Her hordes are routed and peace and harmony rule among the gods while the work of further creation continues.

Tiamat appears in different cultures with a variety of spellings, such as Tiawath, the Tohu of the Hebrews and the Tauthe of the Syrians. The most common elements are that she represents the feminine principle of creation and is symbolized in the form of a dragon or serpent.

Serpents appear in most any mythology as symbols of power over life and death, chaos or just the ever popular adversary. It is often symbolic of sex in relation to its phallic associations, or of the underworld as many serpents find their homes under the ground.

In some cultures, including Hebrews at the time of Moses and the American Indian tribes, believers have allowed themselves to be bitten by poisonous snakes to symbolize healing or spirituality. It is a test of faith that requires surviving the effects of the poison. The Ophites, a Gnostic sect of Christian association, are well known for serpent mythology. There were some Ophite sects who vilified Jesus, associating him with the serpent, and other sects who cursed him as the enemy of the serpent. Both are known for using live serpents in their ceremonies and allowed the serpents to crawl over their bread in order to consecrate it.

The serpent of the Old Testament is the best known example of serpent symbolism used to represent the adversary. In Genesis, the serpent instructs Eve to partake of the fruit of the tree of knowledge of good and evil, which has been forbidden by their creator (Sun) god. Eve succumbs to the temptation, and also gives some of this fruit to Adam. This action is followed by disruptive chaos. Adam and Eve are evicted from their happy paradise and make to suffer for their new found knowledge. The serpent becomes the first god of chaos (in this particular mythology), representing rebellion against the order of ignorance imposed by an all-powerful god.

Choronzon is gaining in popularity in recent years as a chaos god, although strictly speaking he is a daemon. He is a dweller in the Abyss, the keeper of the gate. He has been known to take form as a black snake, jackal or fox. Chronzon suffers from a bad reputation, yet his employment as keeper of the gate is something to be considered. The gate of the Abyss keeps the souls of the dead in, as well as the souls of the living out. Modern writings referring to Choronzon appear in the works of Michael Bertiaux and Aleister Crowley, as well as in Kenneth Grant's writings about these two well known magicians. Older references to Choronzon are difficult to locate. The first traceable written reference to him is in the writings of the well known magician, John Dee. The reason for this lack of early reference to Choronzon was explained to me by a very Wise magician at a social event in a London bookshop in March of 1992.

The very nature of Choronzon is non-linear, as is the nature of chaos itself. Even as my own linear thinking processes scramble to categorize this god with the others, as having a beginning in a specific geographical mythology and the subsequent story to explain his creation and purpose, the nature of Choronzon is such that he simply exists, without beginning or end, and continues to be a tricky force to conjure during a ritual. Choronzon is often referred to as a daemon rather than a god, which explains his absence from many texts of early pantheons. He has had his cults though, generally worshipping him in his guise as the Black Snake who guards the portal between this world and the 'other'.

It is difficult to draw a definite line between what makes a god chaotic or just 'dark', or 'evil'. Some mythologies keep the question of good and evil apparently simple, like the eskimos who have only two gods. Pirksama is good, and Angakok is evil. So why is it that the witch doctors are always named after Angakok? The power of life and death, healing or suffering, is a thing of fear to many peoples. Once again, the unknown chaos of life and death is associated with fear and superstition.

Many of these supposedly evil gods have a purpose beyond just creating misery and havoc among poor mortals. For example, Huwawa is a Babylonian god, who happens to be the son of Pazuzu, who in turn is best known for his role in The Exorcist as the possessing demon, who has a particularly nasty disposition. Huwawa is the guardian of cedar forests. Somehow that sounds like a worthwhile occupation, if not as devastatingly important as guardian of the gate of the Abyss.

The most common thread in these stories about gods and chaos is their representation of creative energy or knowledge of the secrets of life and death. These things have been forbidden to mere mortals in the majority of cultures. What often goes unnoticed when the Sun god comes along to liberate the mortals from the 'evils' of the chaos gods, is that the sun god then sets himself up as ruler over the mortals. The new ruling god will go on to demand blind faith and obedience from his subjects, while his priest class will keep the common people in obedience by frightening them with horrid tales of evil about the adversary, who was likely worshipped in a creative capacity in an earlier version of the same culture.

Our modern western culture is more aware of the symbolism in old mythological tales and people are less likely to believe in the actual personifications of gods and goddesses. Modern psychoanalysis takes the place of many of the old rituals to god-forms in working out the needs of individuals. As scientists learn more about the actual workings of the universe, we see the same concepts mirrored in simple shapes and forms such as spirals and serpentine water flows as in the mythologies common to most peoples.

The one question which has eluded scientists in this century has been the basis of creation itself. Despite theories of the formation of the universe that become generally accepted in the scientific community, the origin of that little spark of life which brings population to the planets, or at least ours, has been out of reach.

It is only very recently that the discoveries of basic principles of chaos science has begun to shed some light on possible answers to this question. In a way, it has become the chaos daemon of the science world.

It seems that the answer to the age-old question of what constitutes good and evil is at least partially answered by the mythologies themselves. That which we do not understand is considered evil, while conformation to whatever the society to which one belongs considers to be normal is good. Renegades and rebels are considered to be evil and yet these same renegades often become the inventors and discoverers of history.

So in examining the roles of chaos gods in history and even in modern times, we find that the question of good and evil becomes more complicated. To conform is considered good, yet leads to stagnation of society. Chaos is associated with new avenues of creation and exploration in both mythology and science. No longer is it the evil daemon of legend, but the hope for the future. Those gods of chaos who are seen as evil were once worshipped as the all powerful creators that their conquerors are now credited to be.

Some modern fiction literature, such as the works of H.P. Lovecraft, is more and more often focusing on a time when these gods of chaos shall again be worshipped and return to power. If one looks at literature as the forerunner of the attitudes of the common people, it becomes apparent that gods are much like kings in that they who are in power are perceived to be good, with the exception of outright tyrants. The short-comings of the ruling entity are often eclipsed by the hopes of the people in the crown prince, or usurper, who is perceived as the new hope for the future.

It seems that in our never-ending quest for knowledge, the human race is returning to the perception that the chaos gods, figuratively of course, are not the villains portrayed by mythology and superstition over the past 2000 years. They are the harbingers of truth and knowledge, the givers of the fruit of the tree of knowledge of good and evil.

Coming back to the modern use of entities in magic, a Chaos Magician may use any god or goddess from any pantheon in a ritual. It is completely dependent on the individual magician, or group practising together, what symbols will hold meaning and communicate the purpose to the subconscious mind. Modern magicians now know that they can create their own gods to serve their purposes. The names are simply a matter of choice. There are many cases where a symbol is chosen from a fictional work, or even an original deity created by the magician expressly for his/her own individual purpose.

The god Cthulhu, from the mythos written by H.P. Lovecraft, is used by magicians quite commonly in modern ritual. There is even a magical Order in existence based on the fictional mythology of this particular series of stories. The members are mostly serious magicians, and understand the concept that their belief in the gods of the mythology (to some extent or other), give them form.

The gods from the *Eternal Champion* series by Michael Moorcock are also somewhat popular among some magicians whose imaginations lean perhaps a bit strongly toward the fictional. This series of novels has a definite polarity between 'chaos' and 'law', with the concept of 'law' representing the classical concept of 'order', opposing chaos.

There are quite a host of deities to represent different aspects of this polarity throughout the stories. Like the mythological deities, these fictional gods, when invoked or evoked in ritual, tend to behave independently according to their nature and can be perhaps more dangerous than their older, mythological counterparts.

Working with Chaos entities is definitely not recommended for inexperienced magicians. As harmless as it may sound, working with fictional or mythological entities can get very much out of control and is not for the dabbler or game-player. There are many horror stories to be heard from teenagers who play at magic, in the spirit of a role-playing game, and are very surprised when something actually happens. Serious magic is for serious magicians who have learned how to stay in control of unpredictable situations.

Having finished my preaching for the day, I would like to mention that I have known experienced magicians who have invoked fictional deities and received spectacular results. Once the magician learns to reconcile the real-but-not-real nature of godforms in his/her own mind, the locus of control is more likely to stay with the magician. However, one must always be aware that these 'imaginary' entities will act apparently independently, and be prepared for unexpected developments. My personal recommendation is to stay with older, established gods and daemons whose nature is well known by the magician.

Fiction can be used in some cases as a model for understanding the nature of magic. The trouble with this is that some people have trouble separating their fictional worlds from reality, and this can lead to all sorts of problems in their daily lives. I once read a wonderful novel called *Godstalk*, by P. C. Hodgell, which gave me a new perspective on pantheism at the time.

The book begins with the main character stumbling into a town at night with all the citizens locked inside their homes to hide from some sort of evil outside. As it turns out, this is the Night of the Dead Gods, when all the gods ever created and forgotten manifest and wander about the town, creating whatever havoc is appropriate. Some, of course, are accustomed to receiving blood sacrifices and actively hunt for victims, which makes it extremely dangerous to be out wandering around town on that particular night.

The point of all this is that the habits of these gods are created by their worshippers. The names, personalities and needs of the assorted gods were created by the humans whom they once served and protected.

In the use of magic, there is no harm in adapting gods or making up new ones. The important thing is to realize that in doing so, we give them form and to be happy with the form we have given them. A personal pantheon could be created by anyone with a minimum of writing talent. All that is required is to establish a list of needs to be filled by god/goddess personalities, and to decide on personalities to fill these needs. Names are open to the far reaches of imagination.

Of course, if everyone created their own gods, there would be more gods than magic users, but the majority of magicians and pagans are able to fill their deity needs with existing pantheons or specific gods and goddesses borrowed from existing pantheons. whatever god-forms one chooses, it is the personal needs of the magic user which must be filled. This constitutes the attitude of the chaos magician toward deity and other entities.

The choice of entities to be brought into ritual or daily life is down to the individual magician, and may even change regularly for specific purposes. The concept of deity itself is seen in the abstract, as something that is belief yet non-belief. It would be easy to classify this as a totally empiric and atheistic viewpoint, but that would not be entirely accurate.

Austin Osman Spare wrote about a concept which he called "neither-neither". This is in reference to something which is neither something or the other. In this case, the entities in question are seen as neither real or not-real. They exist for us, yet do not exist. We give them existence in our belief, which is a very real existence. Yet if we choose not to believe in them, they do not exist, unless perhaps another magician has chosen to believe in a particular entity and we come into contact with it through a common experience with the other magician. Then, if there is a conflict of interests, the existence of the entity can depend on the strength of belief or non-belief of the individual magicians concerned. This begins to sound like a tacky horror film with a war brewing between rival magicians.

It is quite real though, and there are many magicians today who have stories to tell about situations which have occurred in their experience through the formation of an entity of their own making or that of another magician. A good example of this is related in the third chapter of *Images and Oracles of Austin Osman Spare*.

Spare was challenged by two visitors to his basement apartment to conjure an elemental to visible appearance. Spare tried to explain to them the difference between generally harmless entities which came from the subconscious to appear at seances and an actual 'intrusive familiar', but they insisted on seeing such a creature.

Spare evoked the entity by drawing a sigil on a white card and holding it to his forehead while muttering the evocation. Within a few minutes, a green mist began to form in the basement apartment, slowly taking shape and developing two black patches, like eyes. The two visitors panicked and begged to have the thing driven away. Spare performed a banishing and the thing faded away, leaving a malevolent atmosphere behind.

Shortly after this incident, one of the visitors died and the other lost his reason. It was Spare's opinion that the entity had been a dissociated part of the subconscious of one of them, which had seized the opportunity to manifest.

This sort of story can be a bit frightening to dabblers in magic, but should serve as a warning to take such things seriously. Understanding the natures of various types of entities is highly recommended before attempting to invoke or evoke anything.

Methods of invocation and evocation are varied in different traditions. The Chaos Magician may use any method of choice, or choose to practice magic without trafficking with elementals or deities at all. There are very few specific magical practices which are indigenous to modern Chaos Magic. They are certainly worth examining, but as has been said more than once in these pages, a Chaos Magician can use any methods which are personally appealing, from any magical tradition or personal invention. There are no limits to creative chaos.

Methods of Chaos

I once read an article in *The Wiccan*, the previous name of a magazine put out by the Pagan Federation in the U.K. (now called *Pagan Dawn*), which was reportedly written by a Chaos Magician. In an attempt to explain the eclecticism of ritual methods used by Chaos Magicians, the author stated that he might be a Wiccan on Monday, a ceremonial magician on Tuesday, a Christian on Wednesday, etc. The article was brought to my attention by a Wiccan friend who was more than a little offended at the cavalier attitude being displayed toward his religion, which he takes very seriously.

I would have to agree that the message could perhaps have been phrased a bit better. Performing a ritual which is associated with a religion is not necessarily the same as believing in the religion. The Chaos Magician may choose to direct his/her belief appropriately to the religion in connection with the ritual, but this still is not the same as belonging to the religion. I will admit to having respect for people who honestly dedicate themselves to a set of beliefs, so long as they do not turn hypocritical or knock on my door trying to sell me their religion or convert me to their views.

The point to make is that a Chaos Magician may adopt a mind-set which allows him/her to perform ritual within the context of any culture or religious practice with which s/he may be admitted to and comfortable with.

Most Chaos Magicians of my acquaintance settle into some form of ritual habits which fall within parameters of their choosing. There is plenty of room for new ideas and methods, but hopping from one set of religious practices to another is more trouble than it is worth. If a Chaos Magician genuinely believes in a religion or philosophy of any kind, it is likely to be incorporated into the practices of that magician.

In groups, some practices become common to the group and spread among solitary magicians if they are committed to writing. One of the practices which are common to most Chaos Magicians is the act of 'banishing' both before and after a ritual. Books on magic will instruct the reader to always banish after a ritual to send away any entities which may be hanging around, but banishing before the ritual as well serves to clear the atmosphere of all sorts of distractions or any stray thought forms which may interfere with the purpose, as well as generally changing the mood for ritual.

A similar effect is achieved when Magicians, Wiccans or other Pagans "ground and center" themselves. Methods of banishing vary greatly. They can include long, drawn out incantations or be as simple as the ringing of a bell. A common banishing for the end of a ritual which has been popularized by members of the IOT is enforced laughter. It tends to clear the air remarkably well.

To Reach the Subconscious

The magical practices which Austin Osman Spare wrote about in his books hold general appeal for Chaos Magicians. Spare, being an artist, was very visually oriented which was reflected in his magical practices. His most often used method for casting a spell was to use a sigil.

Spare's method was rather simple and direct. It consists of writing out the intent of the magician, choosing the exact words carefully to reflect a positive thought process. For example, rather than say, "I wish that I was not afraid of heights", one might say, "I wish that I will feel confident in high places". This method is even more effective if the magician has his/her own magical alphabet which can be used. The next step is to cross out all repeating letters, so if we use the above intent, this process would leave us a series of letters as follows; Iwshtalfecondgp. From these letters, the magician creates a graphic design as s/he pleases. This is the symbol which represents the desire. A pictorial design may be used for this purpose just as effectively, so long as the design is sufficiently abstract in the mind of the magician.

The sigil then has to be charged, or "reified". there are many ways to do this, but the important thing to realize is that the idea is to implant the intent into the subconscious mind and subsequently forget it with the conscious mind. This can be a little tricky. The easiest and most popular method of accomplishing this is through sexual release. Strong emotions are quite valuable in the practice of magic. Sexual orgasm is relatively easy to obtain and less potentially erratic than using something like anger or fear.

To charge the sigil sexually, one concentrates on the sigil while being brought to orgasm either through auto-

Top: Spare's example of a sigil to give himself the strength of a tiger.
Bottom: Example of a design made from ordinary alphabet letters. A
different design could be made from an alphabet known only to the
magician, or a drawing which depicts the magician's desire

eroticism or with the help of a partner. It is important to remember that this is an act of magic rather than a sexual experience. Losing concentration and giving oneself over to physical impulses will result in failure of the ritual. At the moment of orgasm, attention should be completely on the sigil design, not the intent. Eyes should be wide open looking at the design.

Afterwards, the sigil design should be either destroyed or put away in a sealed container for additional charging at a later date, and a banishing performed followed by complete distraction in some mundane activity. This will help in the process of consciously forgetting the intent, which can be the most difficult part.

Austin Osman Spare was known to draw sigils on parchment and seal them into a crucible which was specially made for sexually discharging himself into, charging the sigil with his own semen. Then, the crucible would be buried and later uncovered for another charging. Many of his spells were accomplished quickly, as described earlier in this book, by simply drawing a sigil on a blank card and holding it to his forehead while muttering some form of incantation, leading to instant results.

Charging can also be accomplished through other means, such as fasting and meditation or similarly to the above method of sexual release, but using other emotions. In his book, *Practical Sigil Magic* (Llewellyn Publications, St Paul, Minnesota, 1990), Frater U.D. suggests using fear by concentrating on the sigil while being terrified on a roller coaster ride. He doesn't recommend it, only suggests it.

Any practice which leads to the spiritual state which Austin Spare called "vacuity" can be applied to charging the sigil. Some are stronger than others, some take longer or shorter times. Spare's methods were designed for his personal solitary use, but groups can do sigil rituals as well.

I once read an article by Ray Sherwin describing a group ritual which included the participants using their bodies to paint a large canvas, creating the visual sigil even as they danced, spinning into the state of vacuity. Chaos methods are wide open to the far reaches of imagination. Only an understanding of the basic concepts is required.

Austin Spare also used a method he called "death postures". This is described in detail in *Practical Sigil Magic*, and can also be found in original form in Spare's Book of Pleasure. The method requires extreme discomfort of the body as well as deprivation of air, creating a sense of 'dying'. It has potential health hazards, and so I prefer to recommend other methods.

Bypassing the conscious mind to reach the subconscious can be done in other ways besides using visual aids. One method, similar in concept to Spare's sigils, is done through a simple verbal chant worked into any ritual. The trick is that the chant is done in a language which the magician, or magicians if it is done in group, do not fluently speak.

Some ceremonial groups use the Enochian language as written by the magician John Dee as a magical language, resulting in a similar effect. It can, however, be done with any language so long as the participants will not easily recognize the words without stopping to translate.

The sentence of intent should be decided on in advance, and carefully worked out through consulting either a written source or someone who speaks the language well.

This must be done without allowing the translation of individual words to become very familiar to anyone who will participate in the ritual.

The sentence is decided, the exact meaning forgotten, then the ritual is conducted in whatever manner the participants choose using the chant repeatedly over and over during at least part of the ritual until the unfamiliar words become difficult to keep repeating and it becomes a struggle just to get the correct syllables out. Then, at a previously agreed on signal, the chanting stops and the ritual is closed with no mention of the intent. Participants move on to some other activity to distract them from thinking about the ritual. Frater U.D. suggests watching television or some other similar activity for the purpose of distraction, and I must agree that this is a good method of completely changing the scene so that the mind does not flow back to the recent ritual.

I must throw in a word of caution here; the exact translation of the sentence in the verbal chant method must be very clear and specific. Some languages have words which can translate a bit differently in context, and possible ways to reinterpret the sentence should be examined. I once did a ritual with this method using Latin.

Being very young and a bit too unfamiliar with the language, I worked out a sentence from a Latin/English dictionary for the purpose of helping a friend who was being blackmailed. The intent was to remove the ability of the person to blackmail my friend by removing a certain object from this person's control. What I didn't realize was that the sentence I came up with could be retranslated to mean, "this house must remain empty".

Five days into the fourteen day ritual, I performed that day's portion of the ritual and went off to work. Later that night I returned to find the house I had been living in completely burned out. I hadn't even lit the intended candle yet. According to witnesses, the place just suddenly exploded into flames, apparently within a short time of when I left. the fire department never determined the actual cause. It was apparently a very hot fire, glass and metal had melted extensively throughout the dwelling.

The only things I was able to sift from the ashes were a few special pieces of my ritual equipment, and some photographs of a very special cat I had once shared by life with, who had been victim of a drunk driver several years earlier. All other photographs in the same box were completely dust, but these were barely singed at the edges, not enough to obscure the image in any way. I still have them. The house was never again occupied.

The moral of this story is: words have power. **Be careful how you use them!**

Chaos Workings

Chaos magic groups have taken to referring to written spells as "workings". Many of these are intended for self-transformation in some manner. This began with members of the IOT and has spread throughout the groups which have formed in anything resembling the image of the original IOT. Generally, workings are created by individuals for a specific purpose which may be used by others, possibly intended for group use or for a purpose of use to other Chaos Magicians. These are quite often based on the principles of magic as written by Austin Spare, Peter Carroll, Ray Sherwin and/or Frater U.D.

Workings are often shared through networking by mail or computer bulletin boards. More recently, some are beginning to be published. The books *Condensed Chaos* (Chaos International, London, 1992) and *Prime Chaos* (Chaos International, London, 1993) both written by Phil Hine include some written workings. these books can be difficult to obtain as books by this author are often released in limited editions. the reader's best chance for acquiring limited edition books of this calibre is to inquire from Atlantis Bookshop, 49a Museum Street, London WC1A 1LY, England.

Any Chaos Magician can write his/her own workings in any format which is appealing to the individual. It is useful to have a written format for ritual work in any group of magicians, for the sake of expedience. A group which practices together regularly can learn specific rituals and co-ordinate their efforts. The solo magician may wish to use a working which someone else has written, an original one, or use spells from other magical paths with a slight mental adaption for the understanding Chaos principles.

My own opinion of the workings I have seen written by other people is that they are generally a bit too formal for my personal taste. Most of them have leaned toward ceremonial magic in structure, which is perfectly fine for many people and no problem for me to adapt to if I am a guest at a ritual. I have not included here any of the specific workings which I have in my files because copyright lies with their authors, who may decide to publish them themselves.

I personally have worked most often alone in recent years and only follow a written ritual if I am visiting a group. On my own, I prefer to generally decide on a progression of events and follow through with it in a spontaneous manner. This would be difficult to adapt for group purposes, although working closely with a partner or very small group who are familiar with each other in ritual can be done with some spontaneity. This sort of spontaneous ritual is most appropriate for the experienced magician. Experience of ritual practice in various forms gives one a feel for the basics of ritual construction.

I generally advise people who are new to magic to seek a Wiccan group which focuses on healing rituals to study with first, and then follow their inclinations as they progress. The reason for this is that Wiccan groups follow a religion which is based on natural magic, and most of them restrict their magical purposes to healing and other very harmless magics which are unlikely to get out of hand. The neophyte can experience the feeling of ritual in such a group and also learn some basic lessons in responsibility. The only problem is that one may fall in with a personality dominated group, of which there are many. The independent thinker may not stay with such a group for long. I can only recommend that in this case, one should try again with another group, and be very wary of anyone who offers to charge you money to teach you magic!

As has been said many times in this book and in other Chaos writings, Chaos Magic can use any and all methods, so long as it works. Learning basic magical techniques is important if one expects to bend those techniques to one's own purposes. As was quoted from a friend's English teacher in reference to another subject; "I don't care if you break the rules of good English, but you've got to know 'em cold if you're going to break them to good effect."

Personal Ritual Structure

As stated earlier, it is common for magicians to become familiar with a general structure which they will most often use in their own rituals. This can vary from one person or group to another greatly. In general, a ritual consists of an opening which would include or be preceded by a banishing, followed by the body of the ritual, then a closing and final banishing. It is the body of the ritual which can vary in content most widely. A ritual may or may not include an invocation or evocation of deity or other ethereal beings. It may include an acting out of "psychodrama" depicting the purpose of the ritual. The entire ritual may center on the construction and charging of a sigil, without recourse to these other possible elements.

This is why the Chaos Magician studies the magics of other paths. The structure of a Wicca ritual is very different from a ceremonial ritual. The Chaos Magician chooses among the known practices of magic. and adds to the mix as imagination requires and allows. Groups will generally fall into a pattern of similar practice. Even the known Chaos groups, with their emphasis on individuality, have become models for imitation.

The solitary magician has more scope for individuality simply because s/he doesn't have to coordinate efforts with anyone else. Yet more often than not, the solitary magician will structure a ritual according to something which was written by someone else. There are few real free thinkers in the world, it is human nature to imitate. In *The Book of Pleasure*, Austin Spare says in the first paragraph of the chapter titled *The Complete Ritual and Doctrine of Magic* "Most emphatically, there is no need of repetition or feeble imitation. You are alive!"

A large percentage of modern Chaos Magicians structure their rituals according to the writings of known Chaos Magicians, who in turn have referred to concepts described by Austin Spare. If one examines the actual writings of Spare, it becomes obvious that the technical language and graphic "models" of magic have been contributed by the modern magicians. Spare worked his complex magic through simple methods, fully understood by himself. Spare's explanations of magical concept have been freely interpreted by different people in their own terms. What is important for the Chaos Magician of today, is to interpret his/her own magic in his/her own way. We can learn a lot from others, but ultimately the magic must come from oneself.

Those who have turned to this chapter looking for specific written rituals will be a bit disappointed. I do not like to write down rituals, and have never performed the exact same ritual twice. While I am quite happy to fit in with the structure of others if I am their guest, I practice my solo rituals in my own manner. This generally consists of an opening/banishing, the body of the ritual, and a closing and banishing. The details vary with each occasion. My daily magics are generally done with no outward performance of ritual at all.

The primary purpose of this book is to simply answer the question. "What is Chaos Magic?" Having been asked to explain it many times, even when I was very new to the subject myself, I felt this book was necessary to explain it. Those who wish to learn more about what (dis)organized Chaos Magicians have to say on the subject are encouraged to read the books listed in the Bibliography or mentioned elsewhere in this book. The magazine, Chaos International is also highly recommended. Information can be obtained from Chaos International, BM SORCERY, London WC1N 3XX, England.

Chaos Magic is not, in itself, a system or philosophy. It is rather an attitude which one applies to one's magic and philosophy. Chaos looks beyond systems and philosophies to the basic physical workings behind magic. To tap the deepest limits of imagination and bring the creative force of primal unformed chaos into one's magical workings is the most straightforward of all magics. Methods and purposes are infinite. The reader is encouraged to study all forms of magic, but to look beyond all that may be read or taught. Creative Chaos has no limits.

BIBLIOGRAPHY

Bray, Christopher *The Collected Works of Austin Osman Spare*, Leeds, U.K.: Sorcerer's Apprentice Press, 1986

Briggs, John & F. David Peat *Turbulent Mirror New York*, NY: Harper & Row, 1989.

Carroll, Peter J. *Liber Kaos* York Beach, Maine: Samuel Weiser, Inc., 1992.

Carroll, Peter J. *Liber Null & Psychonaut* York Beach, Maine: Samuel Weiser, Inc., 1987.

Drury, Neville *Dictionary of Mysticism and the Occult* New York: Harper and Row, 1985.

Frater U.D. *Practical Sigil Magic* St. Paul, MN; Llewellyn Publications, 1990.

Gleick, James *Chaos: Making A New Science* New York, NY; Viking Penguin Inc., 1987.

Grant, Kenneth *Images and Oracles of Austin Osman Spare* London: Frederick Muller Limited, 1975.

Hamilton, Edith *Mythology* Boston: Little, Brown and Company, 1942.

Hitching, Francis *Earth Magic* New York. NY: William Morrow & Company, Inc., 1977

Peat, F. David *Synchronicity: The Bridge Between Matter and Mind* New York, NY; Bantam Books, 1987.

Rehmus, E.E. *The Magician's Dictionary* Los Angeles, CA: Feral House, 1990.

Sherwin, Ray *The Theatre of Magick* Morton Press, 1978.

Index

FREE DETAILED CATALOGUE

A detailed illustrated catalogue is available on request, SAE or International Postal Coupon appreciated. Titles are available direct from Capall Bann, post free in the UK (cheque or PO with order) or from good bookshops and specialist outlets. Title currently available include:

Animals, Mind Body Spirit & Folklore
Angels and Goddesses - Celtic Christianity & Paganism by Michael Howard
Arthur - The Legend Unveiled by C Johnson & E Lung
Auguries and Omens - The Magical Lore of Birds by Yvonne Aburrow
Book of the Veil The by Peter Paddon
Call of the Horned Piper by Nigel Jackson
Cats' Company by Ann Walker
Celtic Lore & Druidic Ritual by Rhiannon Ryall
Compleat Vampyre - The Vampyre Shaman: Werewolves & Witchery by Nigel Jackson
Crystal Clear - A Guide to Quartz Crystal by Jennifer Dent
Earth Dance - A Year of Pagan Rituals by Jan Brodie

Earth Magic by Margaret McArthur
Enchanted Forest - The Magical Lore of Trees by Yvonne Aburrow
Healing Homes by Jennifer Dent
Herbcraft - Shamanic & Ritual Use of Herbs by Susan Lavender & Anna Franklin
In Search of Herne the Hunter by Eric Fitch
Inner Space Workbook - Developing Counselling & Magical Skills Through the Tarot
Kecks, Keddles & Kesh by Michael Bayley
Living Tarot by Ann Walker
Magical Incenses and Perfumes by Jan Brodie
Magical Lore of Animals by Yvonne Aburrow
Magical Lore of Cats by Marion Davies

Magical Lore of Herbs by Marion Davies
Masks of Misrule - The Horned God & His Cult in Europe by Nigel Jackson
Mysteries of the Runes by Michael Howard
Oracle of Geomancy by Nigel Pennick
Patchwork of Magic by Julia Day
Pathworking - A Practical Book of Guided Meditations by Pete Jennings
Pickingill Papers - The Origins of Gardnerian Wicca by Michael Howard
Psychic Animals by Dennis Bardens
Psychic Self Defence - Real Solutions by Jan Brodie
Runic Astrology by Nigel Pennick
Sacred Grove - The Mysteries of the Forest by Yvonne Aburrow
Sacred Geometry by Nigel Pennick
Sacred Lore of Horses The by Marion Davies
Sacred Ring - Pagan Origins British Folk Festivals & Customs by Michael Howard
Secret Places of the Goddess by Philip Heselton
Talking to the Earth by Gordon Maclellan
Taming the Wolf - Full Moon Meditations by Steve Hounsome
The Goddess Year by Nigel Pennick & Helen Field
West Country Wicca by Rhiannon Ryall
Witches of Oz The by Matthew & Julia Phillips

Capall Bann is owned and run by people actively involved in many of the areas in which we publish. Our list is expanding rapidly so do contact us for details on the latest releases. We guarantee our mailing list will never be released to other companies or organisations.

Capall Bann Publishing, Freshfields, Chieveley, Berks, RG20 8TF.